The Oriental 7-Day Quick Weight-Off Diet

NORVELL

Parker Publishing Company, Inc.

West Nyack, New York

Library of Congress Cataloging in Publication Data

Norvell.
    The oriental 7-day quick weight-off diet.

    1. Reducing diets. 2. Cookery, Oriental.
I. Title.
RM222.2.N67   613.2'5   75-12553
ISBN 0-13-642116-4

Printed in the United States of America

Also by the author:

Norvell's Dynamic Mental Laws for Successful Living (1965)
Meta-Physics: New Dimensions of the Mind (1967)
Cosmic Magnetism: The Miracle of the Magic Power Circle (1970)
Mind Cosmology (1971)
Occult Sciences: How to Get What You Want Through Your Occult Powers (1971)
The Miracle Power of Transcendental Meditation (1972)
One Hundred Thousand Dollar Dream and How to Make It Come True (1973)
Universal Secrets of Telecosmic Power (1974)

FOREWORD

I have long known and admired NORVELL for his honest opinions regarding the true philosophy for a healthy, happy and prosperous life.

In the thirty years that I have been his personal physician, NORVELL has regularly appeared for check-ups, and I have marveled at the fact that he seems to retain a youthful resiliency and health that is beyond his 65 years.

I ascribe this amazing vitality and youthful life energy to his remarkable philosophical approach to life and to whatever he has followed as his dietary and health regime throughout these years.

I am delighted that now, at last, NORVELL has again presented to the public an excellent and thorough book on the Oriental system of living, thinking, dieting and meditating, which is bound to benefit the lives of the thousands who will study it. His book, *The Oriental 7-Day Quick Weight-Off Diet,* has in it many of the most scientific and advanced thoughts of our age, as well as reflecting the wisdom and life habits of the Ancients. NORVELL is a deep student of the Mystical, as well as the modern scientific methods for maintaining health, happiness and peace of mind.

In my many years as a physician and surgeon, I have seen the results of careless dietary habits, which have often led to disease and shortened life. In the modern age more and more physicians are coming to realize the vital importance of diet in relation to maintaining the body at a peak of health and energy.

NORVELL seems to have captured in this book some of these latest scientific methods for not only controlling the body's weight, but for keeping it in good health, with a maximum amount of energy and well-being.

More and more physicians are realizing the health hazards that arise from being overweight and any attempt to reduce this hazard is welcomed by the medical profession. It certainly makes our task easier when people learn the rules for nutrition and health through proper breathing, exercising, dieting and thinking.

I believe NORVELL has captured, in his book, the elusive secret for helping people maintain their body health for many long years and it will, I am sure, be welcomed by his large reading public as another milestone in his magnificent career in which he has brought health, happiness and peace of mind to millions.

I heartily recommend this book to all those who are searching for a better way of life.

W. Spencer Gurnee, M.D., F.A.C.S.

Introduction

It is estimated that more than 80 million Americans are overweight. The problem has reached epidemic proportions, and physicians, psychiatrists and sociologists are alarmed at the catastrophic results that ensue in increased illness and premature death to millions of people.

Diseases due to obesity now account for more than half the annual deaths in this country. Such ailments as arteriosclerosis, high blood pressure, heart failure, diabetes, arthritis and many others, take their toll in human lives and shorten the life span by as much as ten to fifteen years.

One of the reasons for this growing problem is that our modern-day technology has reached a point where we use machines to do the labor that was formerly done by human beings. The caloric requirements of the average daily worker today are considerably lower than when we were an agricultural race, and the energy requirements are much lower.

Despite this fact, most people in America are still operating on the heavy laborer's diet of meat, potatoes, gravy, bread, cake, pie and heavy animal fats.

The human body with its low energy-expenditure simply cannot take such a heavy diet. The caloric intake for the average American runs from 2,700 calories for women, to as much as 3,000 to 4,000 calories for men.

When you compare this heavy caloric intake with that necessary to reduce, which is from 900 to 1,200 calories a day, you must realize that people cannot lose weight nor maintain health under the present system of dieting.

WHY THE ORIENTAL 7-DAY MIRACLE DIET WORKS

In the Orient, China, India, Japan and other Eastern countries, there are few fat people. The people work far harder than in our Western world, and they consume fewer calories per day. They suffer less from high blood pressure, heart disease, arthritis, and hardening of the arteries. Their diet is simple and yet their expenditure of energy is tremendous.

My Oriental 7-day miracle diet is based on my scientific research in which I investigated the diets in these countries, as well as the diets of those living in other parts of the world, which are similar. In the Andes, it was reported in the newspapers, there are people who follow a diet similar to that which I give in this book. These people have a diet that consists almost entirely of vegetables, grains, fruits and little meat protein. Their animal fat-intake is as low as 60 grams a day, whereas the average American fat-intake is usually around 450 grams a day!

This race of people in the Andes live to be from 110 to 145 years of age, and seldom die of heart trouble or our modern American diseases.

The Orientals practiced this form of dieting for centuries and their diet is restricted mostly to rice and vegetables. Occasionally they eat fish, poultry and meat, but in areas where meat and poultry were difficult to obtain, these people in China, India, Japan, and other Far Eastern countries often worked all day in the fields, and were sustained by a simple diet of rice, vegetables, grains and nuts. When they were hungry they ate all they wanted of their simple fare, and yet they seldom became fat. Their bodies were healthy and gave them tremendous energy.

In my lengthy study of the methods used by millions of people in the Far East in their diet habits, I found that the very simplicity of their diets kept them from gaining weight and yet, they had sufficient energy to meet their daily work requirements.

In formulating my Oriental 7-day miracle diet for losing weight, I have modified it to suit the needs of twentieth century working men and women, who need not only lose weight, but who must have the energy that will sustain them in the rigorous life of our twentieth century of stress and strain.

WHY MOST PEOPLE CANNOT DIET SUCCESSFULLY

Most people hate to diet because they are deprived of all the foods that give them pleasure in most reducing diets. People dislike any diet plan that makes them feel perpetually hungry.

Hunger is nature's way of warning us that the body mechanism requires nourishment to sustain the life function. It is subconsciously alarming when a person feels hunger pangs. His first instinct is to eat until the hunger pangs go away. This usually means eating the things that most quickly satisfy the appetite.

The foods that give stomach satisfaction and quick energy are the carbohydrate foods: starches, sugars, and fats. These satisfy hunger immediately but they are quickly converted by the body into stored energy or excess fat.

It is much more satisfying to the taste buds to feast on ice cream and cake than to eat proteins, grains and vegetables for the carbohydrates give taste satisfaction that the proteins and vegetables do not give. However, these carbohydrates call on the body to store the excess energy, producing fat, and soon the person is hungry once again and continues the vicious cycle of eating to satisfy his hunger pangs.

THE 7-DAY MIRACLE DIET
DOES AWAY WITH HUNGER!

The wonderful thing about the 7-day Oriental miracle diet is that it does away with hunger pangs entirely! This should be the first requirement in any adequate diet that will properly nourish the body and yet give a sense of satisfaction to the person who is trying to reduce.

A woman I once knew was unhappy in her marriage and ate her way to 210 pounds in a year's time. She could not stop eating candy and other sweets. She began to gain weight and the more she gained the more she ate to keep up the body fat.

When she came to me for advice, she had already lost her husband's love and he was running around with other women. Out of desperation this woman decided to try the 7-day miracle diet. The first thing she did was to establish the fact she would not be hungry during the dieting that would, in her case, require several months. When she found that with this diet she could eat as much as she wanted of certain foods, she was delighted, and thus one of the most serious mental blocks was overcome.

In this woman's case she continued the diet beyond the 7-day period, for her weight was so great she could not lose sufficient weight in that first week. But within one year's time she was back to her normal weight of 130 pounds and not only won back her husband's love but felt better than ever before. She was then put on a sustaining diet to keep her weight at normal.

The 7-day Oriental miracle diet will give you the following benefits immediately:

1. You will be able to lose as much weight as you wish, easily and quickly, without much effort on your part and without having to starve yourself. You will be able to eat all the food you want, as much as four or five pounds a day and you will feel constantly full and satisfied.

2. You will be given a variety of good and nourishing foods that are tasty and, without counting calories, will give you the illusion you are constantly stuffed. This will help remove the subconscious alarm bell that rings when most people try to diet, and which makes them keep eating the quick-energy producing foods that make fat. These foods do not sustain the body's energy and fail to keep the blood sugar content at high levels, which are required for steady energy outputs.

3. You will be able to eat not just three square meals a day, but as many as six or eight! In other words, you will eat as often as you wish and whenever you feel hungry. This food intake will be the type that does *not* go to fat.

4. While you are on the Oriental 7-day miracle diet you will have a sense of well-being. This is psychologically important, for most people cannot remain on a reducing diet for any length of time, because they become irritable and feel a sense of nervousness, which makes them turn to food as a source of consolation.

The foods on the 7-day miracle diet will remove that sense of irritability by making you feel full and satisfied. The resulting psychological benefits will be such that you will have a sense of well-being constantly.

5. On the 7-day miracle diet you can eat a wide variety of foods that give you perfect nourishment. These foods will also

help satisfy your hunger urge. You can eat most lean meats, fish, eggs, cheese and milk products, cottage cheese, yogurt and vegetables, as well as certain types of fruits.

6. This 7-day miracle diet will give you a proper, balanced nutrition that makes it possible for you to do a full day's work, with more energy than ever before. You will seldom feel tired and lazy, as you may when you are stuffed with the wrong types of carbohydrates, starches and fats. The reason for this is that this diet will give you all the necessary carbohydrates, proteins, vitamins and minerals your body requires for perfect health. This diet will not only cause you to reduce to your correct weight but when you continue on your weight-sustaining diet, you will not put on the weight that you have lost. This is the error in most quick-reducing plans!

7. You will be given a list of "negative energizer" foods to eat that actually help burn away the body fat. These foods will reduce you because they require more energy to digest than they give to the body. This means that the more of these reducing foods you eat, the more weight you will lose!

If you ate nothing for a period of ten days, you would lose only about a pound a day. But if you eat these reducing foods on this list, you will lose as much as two pounds a day! This is the secret behind the Oriental 7-day reducing diet—the more you eat of these special foods, the more you lose, for it takes more calories to digest these foods than they give to your body!

8. With this 7-day miracle diet you will actually begin to lose from one to two pounds a day immediately. If you happen to be only ten pounds overweight—the 7-day miracle diet is sufficient and requires little effort or will power on your part.

However, if you happen to be from 20 to 50 pounds overweight—or even more, you need not stop at the end of the seven days, but you can continue for a period of three or four weeks, eating all the food you want, and still burning up the body fat until you reach your required, normal weight.

9. After you have lost the pounds you want, you will then go on a sustaining diet that will be followed the rest of your life. This diet will keep you slender, give you great energy and constantly keep you at the weight you desire.

However, if you binge occasionally and put on a few pounds, the 7-day miracle diet can be used again and you will quickly lose the undesired pounds. This will remove the psychological fear that you are going to get back the lost pounds and be as fat as you were before. When you once know that you can go on a corrective diet for only a few days, you will no longer fear dieting.

10. In this 7-day miracle diet you will be given a variety of tasty menus that are nourishing and which make you feel you are not really dieting but trying new and delicious recipes. You will learn exotic dishes from the Orient that you can add to your regular diet and which will make you a gourmet cook with little effort or expense.

11. In this 7-day miracle diet you are *not* denied the fat producing foods, which are generally more delicious than typical dieting foods. These fat producing foods such as meat, fish, cheese, milk and eggs furnish the body with calories that are quickly turned into fat. This is why diets that tell you to eat as much as you wish of meat, eggs and cheese are faulty. However, in this diet, you will learn how to mix these fat-producing foods with the weight-reducing foods, such as vegetables, grains and fruits, and as it requires more calories to digest these foods than the body receives in energy, these foods will make you lose weight safely and quickly.

12. The reason why this 7-day Oriental miracle diet works so beautifully is that you are psychologically conditioned to the fact that it is simple to follow and that there are no mental or physical hazards. The reason why so many people cannot stick to a diet is that they feel it is a dreary and long drawn-out chore which will tax them mentally and physically.

In this 7-day miracle diet we use the same principle that guides alcoholics in their fight to free themselves from overdrinking—they go without alcohol one day at a time, until they gain such strength that they can do without a drink for days or months.

It is easy to visualize yourself cutting down on food for a period of only one week. In fact, it is fun, for there is sufficient food intake to keep you from ever growing hungry and then by the end of the seven days, when you see the dramatic results, your willpower is so strengthened that you can continue the 7-day diet for another seven days—or as many more as you require to get you down to your normal weight.

NORVELL

CONTENTS

— 1 —

The Natural Oriental Diet for Losing Weight Without Hunger

Through the natural Oriental diet, which is the basis of my 7-day diet plan to reduce without hunger, you can begin to lose weight from the very first day without any effort on your part and without the hunger pangs usually associated with dieting that leads people to give up after a few days.

Then, when you have lost your desired pounds, you can keep your weight at normal through a pleasant, safe and effortless diet that has been used by millions of people in the Far East for centuries.

On this 7-day miracle diet you can have a maximum degree of efficiency, continue your work and enjoy a perfectly normal life while you follow this diet. There will be no periods of weakness, depression, nervousness, headaches or other symptoms which usually follow most efforts to reduce. This is because you can avoid the gnawing hunger pangs that usually accompany most weight-reducing diets. You do this by eating as many of the weight-reducing foods on our diet as you wish, at any time you feel hungry, and you need not fear that they will be converted into unwanted fat!

17

WHY MOST PEOPLE CANNOT DIET SUCCESSFULLY

Most people hate to diet because they are deprived of most of the foods that give them pleasure in their daily diets. People dislike any diet plan that makes them feel perpetually hungry.

Hunger is nature's way of warning us that the body mechanism requires nourishment to sustain the life function. When a person feels hunger pangs it rings a subconscious bell that causes him to want to immediately satisfy the urge to eat. The first instinct is to eat until the hunger pangs go away. This usually means eating the fat-producing foods that most quickly satisfy the appetite.

The foods that give stomach satisfaction and quick energy are the carbohydrate foods: starches, sugars and fats. It is true that these foods satisfy the hunger urge immediately but they are quickly converted into stored energy or excess fat!

It is much more satisfying to the taste buds to feast on ice cream and cake than to eat proteins, grains and vegetables. The carbohydrate foods give fast satisfaction that the proteins and vegetables do not give. However, these carbohydrate foods call on the body to store the excess energy and the body converts these foods into fat. Very quickly the person feels hungry again and the cycle of eating to satisfy hunger pangs continues.

THE 7-DAY MIRACLE DIET DOES AWAY
WITH HUNGER PANGS!

The wonderful thing about my 7-day Oriental miracle diet is that it does away with hunger pangs entirely! This should be the first requirement in any adequate diet that will properly nourish the body and yet give a sense of satisfaction to the person who is trying to lose weight.

I once knew a woman, Thelma R., who had marital problems and soon ate her way to 210 pounds. She could not stop eating candy and nibbling on cakes and cookies between meals. The more weight she gained the more she ate to keep up the body fat.

When Thelma R. came to me for advice on her problem, she told me her husband had ceased loving her and was running around with other women. To win back her husband's love Thelma wanted to get back to her normal weight, so she began my 7-day miracle diet with great enthusiasm.

The first thing she did was to establish the fact that she would not be hungry during the dieting period. In her special case, as she was so very much overweight, I knew that it would take several weeks for her to get back to her former, normal weight. When I told Thelma that she could eat as much as she wanted of certain foods and never again feel hungry, she was delighted, and thus one of the most serious mental blocks to reducing was removed.

It took Thelma R. several weeks to lose the 80 superfluous pounds and once again reach her former weight of 140 pounds. Then she was put on a sustaining diet to keep her weight stabilized at normal. By using the same techniques she had learned in the reducing diet, she could still satisfy her taste buds and eat all she wanted of certain foods, never again suffering from hunger pangs. But what was most important to this woman, she was able to win back her husband's love and respect. He stopped running around with other women and became a faithful and loving husband once again.

Not only is it vitally important to eat a balanced diet, even while reducing, but it is even more important that you build a mental philosophy which can keep your mind calm and controlled during your period of dieting, so you can absorb the nutrients necessary to keep the body healthy and normal during your stringent period of dieting.

To prove the importance of maintaining a high level of energy through a balanced diet even when you are reducing, an experiment was conducted by nutrionists recently. They put a group of ten young women on a stringent diet. They were given overcooked vegetables from which all nutrients were removed. They were given white bread and white sugar and allowed to eat pastries, canned fruits in heavy syrup, ice cream and cake and other heavy carbohydrate foods. All fresh vegetables and salads were eliminated from the diet and they were not allowed to eat any form of protein, such as meat, cheese or milk products. Even eggs were prohibited.

On this restricted diet, within two weeks, these normally healthy young women became fatigued, nervous and neurotic. They quarreled over trifles; they lost any desire to do any kind of work. The more they ate of this restricted diet, the worse they became until some of them actually seemed to be psychotic.

When these women were put back on a normal diet of fruits, vegetables and balanced proteins, these young women recovered from their symptoms and had their former feelings of well-being and energy without fatigue, irritability and lassitude. Another important effect was that the tendency to overeat, which came with their predominantly carbohydrate diet, began to add pounds to their weight and only when they returned to their normal diets did they begin to stabilize their weight.

PROTEINS IMPORTANT IN ANY REDUCING PLAN

In my study of the diet problems of most overweight people I discovered that they ate plenty of food, but it was mostly of the wrong kind. They ate the denatured, overcooked, fattening foods that gave them bulk but were lacking in nourishment.

It is vitally important in any weight-reducing diet that there is sufficient protein to meet one's daily needs. This is determined by the expenditure of energy in a day's work. Obviously, a sedentary worker requires fewer calories than a laborer. Although with the Oriental 7-day miracle diet we do not count calories, it is important to know about calories and to avoid taking in too many calories while on the reducing plan. At least 60 grams of protein daily is essential to proper nourishment.

This daily intake of protein assures the body of getting enough nourishment to supply the requirements for vitality and energy. We take into account the fact that the body requires this protein intake every day, even while reducing. This is especially true for those who are past 40, when the body requires certain proteins and amino acids which are essential to proper nourishment. Without these amino acids, furnished by proteins, the body cannot manufacture the proper enzymes that affect metabolism and which give the body nourishment. This is why many people feel so fatigued while they are dieting and cut down on the vitally essential protein foods.

Also, with my 7-day Oriental diet you will avoid another serious dietary deficiency—the serious drop in blood sugar that most dieters experience when they go on a drastic weight-reducing program.

On this 7-day miracle diet you can eat all you want of nonfattening foods and you need never experience hunger. You may eat as much as six times a day and still lose your quota of two pounds a day!

THE ORIENTAL SYSTEM OF DIETING CLEANSES THE BODY OF TOXIC POISONS

One of the reasons why the Oriental system of dieting works to reduce, as well as to maintain perfect health afterwards, is because most of the foods used in this diet are fresh, vital foods—vegetables, grains and fruits, which help keep the body in a state of alkalinity and which flush out the poisons that gather in the body through toxic wastes and the heavy carbohydrate foods. This diet helps furnish the glands with the correct nutrients which will cause them to function more efficiently and to do the job for which they were intended.

Drugs should be taken only with a physician's advice. They often tend to overstimulate the glands of the endocrine system, until finally they are no longer able to perform their function and the entire system collapses.

In some cases eating stimulating foods or drinking too much coffee or alcohol, or filling the system with salt, sugars, starches and other concentrated forms of highly irritating foods gives a temporary acceleration of the entire glandular system, causing them to oversecrete and become exhausted. Then they fail in their vital functions with fatal results.

A Woman Suffered from Overstimulated Glands

The case came to my attention of Lillian P., a woman who was very much overweight—about 50 pounds. She suffered severe arthritis, high blood pressure and other ailments that kept her constantly sick. She told me she drank from eight to ten cups of coffee a day. She needed its stimulus to keep her going during the day. Then at night, despite the fact that she was exhausted, she was so highly nervous and tense that she couldn't sleep. She then took sleeping pills to help her rest. Finally she was taking so many sleeping pills that they ceased to be effective. With her doctor's cooperation, I told her first to give up coffee and drink a caffein-free substitute. Lillian went on the Oriental diet, using no meat whatsoever for the first two weeks. Within three weeks' time Lillian had lost 30 pounds, her distressing symptoms began to disappear and the pain in her joints was considerably reduced.

Most overweight people have unnaturally high blood pressure and their heart action is often abnormal. If it is necessary to walk up a flight of stairs, or move rapidly, they feel sluggish. This is because their glands and internal organs function sluggishly. When the weight is once again reduced to normal these symptoms usually disappear in a few short days.

During this 7-day miracle Oriental diet, many people who suffered from diabetes regularly checked with their doctors and it was found that they experienced a drastic reduction of blood sugar! Patients who had high blood cholesterol levels when they were overweight showed dramatic reductions of this condition and returned to near-normal in a short space of time, while following this 7-day miracle reducing diet.

For centuries the world has known of the Oriental 7-day miracle diet, without realizing that it could be used for losing weight as well as to sustain a person in perfect health and with normal weight the rest of his life.

Man is, by nature, herbivorous and could actually subsist on a diet of vegetables, grains, fruits and milk products. Thousands of Americans are vegetarians and do not eat meat of any kind and yet they are in splendid health, with few of the health complications we find in those who eat too much meat. Vegetarians are seldom overweight; they usually have tremendous vitality and often live to be a hundred years or more.

George Bernard Shaw, the great dramatist, was a vegetarian most of his life and he lived to be nearly 100 years old. He did his greatest work after he reached the age of 60 and he was spry, active and had tremendous mental and physical energy. He claimed that his diet kept him in this condition.

Mahatma Gandhi was a vegetarian most of his life also, and when he was assasinated, even though he was in his early seventies the doctors said that his body was like that of a man in his thirties. Gandhi used certain principles of our Oriental diet, and was famous for his long fasts, where he ate no solid foods for days and subsisted only on diluted orange juice and water.

MEAT PRODUCTS VALUABLE SOURCES OF PROTEINS

The 7-day Oriental miracle diet for losing weight does not advocate eliminating meat from the diet entirely. In our western world we seem to require the important amino acids and other elements furnished by meat products. But those who are vegetarians and do not wish to eat red-blooded meats may live a long and healthy life by substituting other proteins such as grains, nuts, soy beans, milk products and rice for meats. Those who are vegetarians, who do not have a weight problem, may want to follow our maintenance diet for the rest of their lives and they can be assured of having a balanced, nutritious diet that will give them health, energy and vigor the rest of their lives.

One Woman Lost 15 Pounds in Two Weeks on This Diet

On this Oriental 7-day miracle diet you may expect to lose from seven to fifteen pounds a week, depending on how rigidly you follow this diet. In the first week the average person loses about ten pounds. Mrs. Jenny T. was 145 pounds when she began this reducing plan. She set her goal at 130 pounds, which she thought was her ideal weight. This was what she weighed when she had married. She had accumulated the extra fifteen pounds over a period of five years and no amount of trying seemed to get rid of it.

Mrs. T. began the 7-day miracle diet after the two day fasting period, which I advocate before beginning the Oriental quick weight loss diet. In that two day period she did lose four pounds, but I explained to her that this was the excess salt and water that was held in her body tissues. Many people will lose much of this excess water on this diet in the first week, which accounts for some of the weight loss. But those who are more than 20 or 30 pounds overweight must stay on the diet a while longer than the seven days so they can safely lose the excess weight without endangering their health.

Then Mrs. T. began the actual Oriental diet and within one week she had lost seven more pounds without effort and without hunger pangs! Because she wanted to lose another four pounds she extended the Oriental diet one more week and easily lost the extra four pounds. Then she went on the normal, maintenance diet, which she maintains to this day. She has reported to me that she has never gained back the lost pounds and that she never felt so good nor had as much energy as she now has. In addition, her clothes now fit her perfectly and she says even her romantic life has been vastly improved since she lost the excess weight and her husband finds her attractive once again.

Now that you understand the basic principles about diet and health, you are ready to embark upon the Oriental miracle diet that can help you shed unwanted pounds, while you retain your vital good health and still enjoy the good things of life.

— 2 —

Taking the First Steps to Lose from Ten to Twenty Pounds Without Effort

The basic foundation of the Oriental 7-day miracle diet is one of natural foods, made up mainly of vegetables, fruits, grains and brown rice, with the addition of fish, fowl or other protein meats. Although rice is thought of as a carbohydrate food, the natural brown rice, which has not been polished, contains many nutrients, including protein, which are valuable as food and which do not convert into fat.

This diet, which includes brown rice, must not be confused with other diets that concentrate only on rice. It is true that rice, when used as an adjunct in a reducing diet, gives that full feeling which helps one resist the tendency to overeat. However, rice alone does not give a balanced nutrition. This is why I have added other foods to our quick reducing system.

For centuries two-thirds of the world's population have lived on a predominantly rice diet. Rice and vegetables, with some meat, fish, milk products and eggs, have been used as the sustaining diet of millions of people in the Far East. You seldom see a fat person in the Far Eastern countries.

I observed in my travels throughout the Far East and India that the rural people who depended solely on the products they raised and did not have access to the processed and refined or canned foods of the cities subsisted entirely on the simple products they were able to raise—mainly, rice, vegetables, fruits, and grains in their natural state.

I checked with medical authorities and hospital records in these countries and discovered a strange thing: Despite the fact that these people knew little about hygienic laws, which accounted for many deaths among children, they often lived to be 100 or more years of age.

The records showed that these people, who lived solely on the natural foods they grew, such as grains and vegetables, had little or no cardiac disease and high blood pressure was practically unknown. There is less cancer, arthritis, sugar diabetes and other diseases, such as high blood-cholesterol, associated with being overweight among these country people.

In my Oriental 7-day diet, I recognize the need of meat proteins. However, I advocate the splendid protein to be found in fish. In fact, the Japanese diet consisting mostly of fish, rice and vegetables, is probably one of the most nourishing of all, for fish have been found to be a better form of protein than the red-blooded meats!

These fine foods, which are nourishing and which are included in my 7-day reducing diet, when eaten as directed, not only cause you to lose weight, but when you have reached your desired normal weight, these same foods, eaten in different proportions, can furnish your body with all the necessary vitamins, minerals and other elements you need in a normal diet. They will also keep you from becoming overweight again. The Japanese are noted for their slender, wiry figures, and seldom do you see an overweight Japanese.

Have you had the experience of eating in a Chinese or Japanese restaurant? After eating several courses consisting of rice, vegetables, soup and lean meat, you felt stuffed and thought you would not want to eat again for days. Then a few hours later you experienced hunger once more and wondered why.

The explanation is simple: you actually receive very little fat-producing food in such an Oriental diet but you do receive plenty of bulk. The egg drop soup has little fat content; the vegetables are mostly boiled; the meat is usually lean and broiled; then when you add three or four cups of tea to the meal, you experienced that stuffed feeling which makes you think you have had a hearty feast. This is one of the reasons for the popularity of the Chinese and Japanese type of restaurant in this country.

My Oriental 7-day miracle diet is based on this basic Oriental diet that extends throughout the Orient, including China, Japan, India, Tibet, Indochina and Vietnam and Cambodia, and also other countries in the Near East and Far East that use rice as their staple diet.

However, to this diet, I have added another important ingredient, which helps you lose weight quickly and without hunger: It is a method of fixing the numerous vegetables that give bulk without giving weight, in a simple manner that requires no special cooking problem and which furnishes you with the bulk that takes away hunger pangs forever.

•

EAT AS MUCH AS YOU WISH AND LOSE WEIGHT!

I promised you that you can, with this miracle diet, *eat as much as you wish and still lose weight.* Also, that you need never be hungry while on this reducing diet. Now let me explain this more fully, before you start on the actual reducing plan.

On this diet, eating the vegetables I shall give you that are nonfattening, it takes more calories to digest these vegetables than they give your body in caloric value. This is one of the secrets of the effectiveness of my 7-day quick weight loss diet.

When a farmer wants to fatten a pig what does he do? He gives him plenty of corn and other fat-producing foods and shuts him up in a small space so he cannot get much exercise, and in a few weeks time he will be fat as a—pig!

THE VITAL IMPORTANCE OF RICE
IN WEIGHT REDUCING

One of the most amazing foods that God has given to man is rice! That vital food can be stored for months without spoiling. It is a staple food that can be grown in most parts of the world. It furnishes the body with many elements that makes it an ideal food where no other food is obtainable.

In extreme cases, a person could live on rice alone indefinitely, without harm to the body. Many of the soldiers in North Vietnam fought ferociously, sustained by only a handful of rice a day, with whatever few vegetables, nuts or berries they could find in the swamps and jungles. The fact they could not be conquered by the well-fed, modern American armies, who subsist on meat, potatoes, bread, sugar, milk, ice cream and pie, attests to the fact that what we consider an adequate American diet may be lacking in the simple, elementary elements that make for good health, stamina and vitality.

Of course, in this 7-day Oriental diet, I do not advocate living on rice alone, for the body needs other vital elements. However, rice in its natural state, before the shell has been removed by polishing, is much more than just another form of carbohydrate; natural brown rice has in it proteins, vitamins and minerals, *which do not add to body weight, but which give the body many nutritional elements needed for even a normal diet.*

By adding vegetables, lean meats, grains, nuts and milk products to this basic food staple, you can actually maintain your body in the peak of condition even after you have reduced to your natural weight.

TWO-DAY FASTING REGIME TO BEGIN
LOSING WEIGHT IMMEDIATELY

To begin losing weight immediately and to convert the foods you eat into solid protein without fat, you should begin your diet regime with the system used in most of the Far Eastern countries: this is to fast for two days and drink only liquids and fruit or vegetable juices. This system of purification of the body is essential before starting to reduce. It will help you rid the body of all accumulated wastes and poisons. It will also help you remove several pounds of excess liquids that may lodge in the body cells, held there by salt that you have eaten for years. If this fasting regime is not followed, the body is not prepared to absorb the new elements introduced into it through the diet and many of the body's previous inflammations and congestions are apt to remain.

I have observed in many of the religious orders of the Far East that the monks observe regular periods of fasting for as long as two or three weeks at a time, with only a daily intake of water, fruit and vegetable juices. Many of these monks live to be more than a hundred years of age and have perfect health, with slender bodies and youthful appearance. Fasting was one of Gandhi's secrets for energy, health and long life.

Follow This Purification and Fasting Regime for Two Days

To begin the purification regime for two days, make it a point to take a glass of water with the juice of a whole lemon when you first arise in the morning. If this is too sour you can flavor it with a touch of honey. This lemon and water will help cleanse the stomach of all mucus and will begin the process of neutralizing the acids which accumulate when you are on an acid-forming diet of starches, sugars and excessive quantities of meat or other proteins.

During the rest of the day you can drink several glasses of fruit juices, without the addition of sugar or other sweeteners. These can be orange, grapefruit, apple or prune juice, or any others that you prefer. You can drink as many as six to eight glasses of these fruit juices a day, but do not eat any solid foods for this two-day period. The natural sugars in the fruit juices are not harmful.

During this two-day fast, whenever you feel hunger pangs take more juice and then drink water in between.

After two days of this juice therapy you will find that you actually do not have much desire for solid foods. Many people have fasted as long as two or three weeks and have had no harmful effects to the body. What happens during these fast periods is that the body is feeding on its own stored fats. However, I do not advocate fasting beyond the two day period. If there is any condition that makes you hesitate in following this two day fast, consult your personal physician as to its advisability. In most cases he will recommend it.

After the second day of fasting you will notice that your sense perceptions are sharper; you will feel a sense of lightness in your body and you will be happier than before. This sense of well-being will permeate everything you do. As you remove the toxic substances that have been poisoning your bloodstream for years, you will experience for the first time in months a general feeling of energy and health.

By the end of the second day of fasting your stomach and other body organs will have had a good rest and will function more efficiently than before.

NOW YOU ARE READY TO BEGIN YOUR WEIGHT-REDUCING PROGRAM

When you have concluded your two-day fasting period you are ready to embark on your regular 7-day reducing regime.

First, I would suggest that you try to rid your diet of regular table salt, which is sodium chloride, and use some of the salt substitutes that are on the market. Salt has the peculiar faculty of holding water in the body tissues and often accounts for from five to ten pounds of excessive weight! More and more nutritionists and doctors are advising against the use of table salt, stressing how it affects the blood pressure and is a prime suspect in many cases of arthritis and other diseases. If there is any doubt in your case, do not hesitate to consult your doctor to see if your condition requires special salt restrictions.

The body needs sodium, it is true, but not sodium chloride, which is labeled as a poison in the drug stores! Sodium is easily obtainable in many of the vegetables we shall use in our reducing diet, including summer squash or zucchini, and green string beans, as well as celery and other green vegetables.

To begin your reducing diet you must eat certain reducing vegetables and avoid the starchy vegetables which add weight to your body.

In dieting to lose weight, you must eat these weight-reducing vegetables each day as a supplement to the other foods given in the reducing list. The easiest and quickest way to utilize these weight-reducing vegetables is to put them into a soup and then eat all the soup you want, as many times a day as you feel hungry. This is why I said that you may eat as much as up to five or six pounds of food a day and eat as often as you feel hungry of these weight-reducing vegetables without putting on an ounce! The vegetables in the list I give below for making the reducing soup take more calories to digest than they give to the body! *The more of these vegetables you eat the more you lose!*

How to Prepare the Reducing Soup

Prepare the following vegetables by cleaning them and cutting them up into a large pot of water.

One head of cabbage.
Six large onions.
A big bunch of celery.
A big green pepper.
A can of whole tomatoes.

After you have cut up these vegetables into medium-sized pieces, cover them over with water and let it come to a full boil. After it has boiled about ten minutes lower the fire and let the reducing soup simmer for a full two and a half to three hours, or until the vegetables are soft. Do not worry that you will be cooking all the nutrients out of the vegetables! This soup is not intended to nourish you! *In fact, if you ate nothing but this soup you would soon starve to death!* It will give no nourishment and no fat to the body whatsoever; that is why it is used, but it will give you the comfortable feeling of being full and you can eat it as often as you wish when you feel hungry, with the other basic reducing foods which I shall give in a few moments. When you eat a bowl of this reducing soup you may sprinkle it with Parmesan cheese to make it more palatable. You can also add a small container of onion soup mix which can be found in your grocery store, just to give it more flavor. This should be done while the big pot of soup is cooking. The reason I suggest preparing a big pot of this reducing soup is that it is easy to prepare and to keep for days in your refrigerator, saving you the bother of making it every day.

To give you full nutritional value on this reducing diet, I shall add other basic foods which will give your body the nourishment you require without adding to your body weight.

This reducing soup is to be eaten between meals and you may also eat your regular three meals a day, and in addition, three or four bowls of the reducing soup, as often as you wish and you will actually lose weight quickly!

The wonderful thing about using this reducing soup is that it will fill you up so much that you will have no feeling or appetite for the carbohydrates and other fat-producing foods. All foods produce fat when they are eaten in large quantities—even lean meats.

Many people believe that eating lean meat and vegetables alone, all they want, will cause them to lose weight. But if they eat more than 900 calories each day they will not lose weight. During this critical 7-day period the actual food intake is kept down to less than 1,000 calories a day. However, you do not need to count calories, as this will be automatic in the quantities suggested in this reducing diet. However, later, I shall have something to say about calories and their importance in adjusting to your regular maintenance diet, after you have shed the unwanted pounds from your weight.

THE BASIC ORIENTAL WEIGHT-REDUCING DIET

Now you are ready to begin the actual basic Oriental weight-reducing diet that will melt the pounds away, so that at the end of seven days you can actually lose as much as ten to fifteen pounds, depending on how rigidly you observe the diet.

The basic element in this 7-day Oriental reducing diet, as I have stated before, is brown rice. The vegetables are eaten in your soup and therefore I shall not include them in planning your three meals a day for the 7-day period you want to lose weight. However, later I shall give you many variations to this rice diet, and many vegetables for the sustaining diet, which are nourishing and tasty, cooked as the Orientals cook them, and these will give you variety in menu planning without adding fat to your body.

FOR BREAKFAST: Start your day with a good solid breakfast. This is one of the most important meals of the day. Many people skimp on breakfast and think they are losing weight; actually this avoiding of a hearty breakfast accounts for many cases of fatigue and headaches and makes people quarrelsome and highly nervous. The reason for this is that during the long period of time while you sleep, the body is without food and this tends to lower the blood sugar level. Upon rising in the morning, after taking a small glass of orange or grapefruit juice, half an hour before your breakfast, you will be much more receptive to a solid breakfast.

Then eat two boiled, poached or fried eggs. Be sure the eggs are fried without grease. The modern coated pans are excellent for greaseless cooking. Then have one piece of whole-wheat toast with margarine, a half spoonful of any kind of jelly or marmalade, and all the coffee you want, if you drink it black and without sugar. However, if you want cream, you may use it but with artificial sweetener. The sugar is more harmful than the cream, for your body needs some fat each day, even when you are reducing. You may take this fat as cream in your coffee or tea, or as margarine on your toast.

Brown rice is not suggested for the morning meal as it is apt to make you feel too full so early in the morning, but it can be used later in the day, either for lunch or for dinner.

If you have breakfast around 7 a.m. you will begin to feel hungry again within a period of three or four hours. Then you can eat a big bowl of the vegetable reducing soup, sprinkled with Parmesan cheese for flavoring. This soup in itself tastes delicious, for the onions give it flavor. Eat as much as you wish or until your hunger pangs go away.

If you go to work and cannot prepare this at home for mid-morning to relieve hunger, you can take a bowl of the vegetable soup in a thermos jug and eat it at your place of business before your regular lunch.

It was found by scientists investigating the food habits of people all over the world that the country people in Bulgaria, Roumania, Yugoslavia, Russia and other Mid-Eastern countries often ate nothing all day but vegetable soup, brown bread, milk and cheese products, yogurt and eggs—with very little meat—and they found that many of these people lived as much as 125 to 135 years of age. They were slender, youthful appearing and often worked in the fields all day up to an advanced old age!

The Importance of Brown Rice

In addition to the reducing soup you are now ready to add the brown rice to your diet. This will be a staple part of your diet while losing weight. Many people think of rice as being starchy, forgetting that the natural brown rice, when it is not ruined by refining and polishing, has valuable proteins and other elements that make it an ideal food.

Prepare a large bowl of brown rice by cooking it with a little salt substitute, for about 45 minutes. If you cannot get brown rice you can use the white rice, although it is not as valuable as a food staple. When the rice is cooked, put it in the refrigerator and twice a day, for lunch and for dinner, warm a small bowlful, about a cup and a half, and add a little melted margarine for flavor. You can eat as much of this rice as you feel gives you a completely satisfied feeling. With the rice you can also eat a four-ounce piece of lean meat, such as veal, beef or lamb, or a piece of chicken with the skin removed, or a piece of chicken broiled or baked. All meats should be broiled or boiled, never fried.

The diet can be varied each day by having a different form of meat. If you are a vegetarian you can eat a meat substitute made from soya beans, or you may use cottage cheese, eggs or skimmed milk.

During this period of dieting eat no cake, pie or ice cream. No desserts of any kind are permitted, except natural fruits or Jello made with natural gelatin and artificial sweetener. This may have fruits added to it, but if they are canned fruits, the syrup should be washed out of them or you may use the canned dietetic fruits that contain artificial sweetener.

You may also eat the following fruits for desserts: stewed apples or apple sauce. You can add a little honey or use artificial sweetener.

You may eat the following fruits with this reducing diet: apricots, prunes, cantaloupe, watermelon, strawberries and cherries. You may also eat honeydew melon and rhubarb. These are the only fruits permitted while on this reducing diet Canta-loupes are wonderful while reducing, for they do not add calories because they require more calories to digest than they give to the body. All the above fruits come in this same category. Other fruits are prohibited while on the weight-reducing diet.

If you feel the need for other desserts while reducing, you may eat fat-free yogurt, which is often mixed with fruit. But remember, yogurt is easily digested and assimilated, so do not overindulge in such foods while dieting!

FOR LUNCH: You are permitted a large serving of cottage cheese with fresh fruit; a salad with a nonfattening salad dressing, which I shall give later; a piece of fish or lean meat, and a piece of whole-wheat bread with a patty of margarine or butter. You may drink coffee or tea, without cream. Or you may use a non-dairy cream with artificial sweetening.

You can satisfy your hunger by adding to this luncheon a bowl of the reducing soup and also a cupful of brown rice, flavored with melted margarine. When you eat this type of lunch, you will have a stuffed feeling, but you have actually eaten nothing that will add fat to your body. To avoid overeating you can take the bowl of reducing soup about an hour or so before lunch or dinner; in this way you will help kill the appetite and will not have a desire for much solid food.

FOR DINNER: Have a bowl of the reducing soup a short time before dinner to kill your appetite. You can then have a helping of one of the meats given above, a small salad of tomatoes, cucumbers and lettuce, and for dessert a bowl of sugar-free Jello, or some fruit, such as applesauce or melon.

Potatoes are not permitted in this reducing diet. However, if you want to add vegetables to this diet and not eat the reducing soup with your dinner, you may have two helpings of any of these vegetables: broccoli, string beans, asparagus, zucchini, spinach, turnips or tomatoes. This gives you a wide variety of the reducing vegetables to eat, if you prepare them without sauces or starchy fillers. They can be steamed until soft and then flavored with a little margarine, or one of the sauces I shall give later that are nonfattening.

FOODS TO AVOID DURING THIS
7-DAY REDUCING PLAN

all white bread
pies and cakes
ice cream
candy
doughnuts
honey (except for flavoring, and limit to one spoonful)
avocado
gravy
jelly and jam
marmalade
mayonnaise
nuts
oil
peanut butter
potatoes
puddings
salad dressings (except as given later)
alcohol of any kind, including wine and beer

HIGH POWER REDUCING VEGETABLES
TO ADD VARIETY TO YOUR MEALS WHILE DIETING

The following vegetables may be eaten during this 7-day reducing diet, for they are all in the category of the reducing type of vegetables that take more calories to digest than they give to the body. You may continue to eat two or three bowls of the reducing soup whenever you feel hungry between meals, and then add variety to your lunches and dinners by using the following vegetables which are not fat-producing.

string beans	asparagus
broccoli	brussel sprouts
cabbage	lettuce
celery	garlic
lettuce	kohlrabi
cucumbers	leek
okra	mushrooms
green peppers	dill pickles

radishes	spinach
watercress	turnips
tomatoes	sauerkraut

While on your reducing food plan you can eat any of the vegetables that grow above ground except peas, corn, and white beans. The only reason these are restricted while on the reducing food plan is that they are heavy in starches and carbohydrates. Later, when on the sustaining diet, these may be added to the regular diet in small quantities.

ONE WOMAN LOST TEN POUNDS
THE FIRST WEEK ON THIS DIET

Arline T. used this basic reducing plan. She did the two-day fasting diet first and immediately lost four pounds. Of course this was mostly water, but water adds up to pounds on your bathroom scales and also shows as puffiness on the body. Then Arline went on the actual Oriental diet of rice and vegetables, with a small piece of lean meat daily for only one week. At the end of that time she had lost the full ten pounds she desired! She did not want to lose more than the ten pounds but when she saw with what ease she could, at will, remove the unwanted pounds Arline stopped fearing dieting and the psychological shock that comes from the belief that we can do nothing to get rid of excessive weight.

From that time on Arline went on her sustaining diet, which I shall give later, and she was able to keep her weight constantly at the level she desired. She felt so good on the rice, vegetables, fruits, grains and little meat, that she persisted in eating the rice long after she had lost her excess weight. She said the rice, eaten at least once daily, seemed to cushion her desire to eat big meals and also it gave her a feeling of being full constantly. Arline also found that the rice satisfied her hunger urge to such an extent that it seemed to substitute for the candies, cakes, ice cream and other carbohydrates which wrecked her diet before. Rice satisfied the carbohydrate craving without adding the dangerous pounds of the other forms of starches, sugars and carbohydrates.

Arline even learned how to prepare rice in various ways,

which I shall give later, and she even used rice for some delicious desserts.

HOW TO USE THE BROWN RICE IN YOUR DIET

You may eat a helping of brown rice, a cupful at least, with margarine on it, at lunch or dinner. This basic staple food will give you a feeling of fullness and help keep you from growing hungry. Sometimes for lunch or dinner you can eat a big bowlful of brown rice with a poached egg on it and a little melted margarine. It will give you tremendous energy and stamina, without that feeling of weakness in the knees that often comes when one is on a stringent, weight-reducing diet.

At the end of the 7-day reducing period, you should actually have lost anywhere from ten to fifteen pounds. The amount varies with different people, for much depends on whether you are extremely active or whether you sit and rest a good deal. If you combine exercise with this Oriental diet, you can easily shed as much as 14 pounds in that 7-day period. This is actually all that most people need to lose to get down to their ideal weight, but there are cases where one needs to lose from 20 to 50 pounds. What then?

If you find that you need to lose more weight after the 7-day period, you can extend this diet to another seven days, always limiting it to one week. This avoids the psychological block that most people face when they must diet over a prolonged period of time. It is like the alcoholic's pledge to stop drinking for only one day at a time.

A case from my files shows how a person can shed more than 50 pounds very easily on this Oriental reducing diet. Mrs. B. had continued to gain weight over the years until she tipped the scales at 185 pounds. Her normal weight for years had been 130 pounds. She was now 45 years of age, and she was feeling fatigue, had symptoms of high blood pressure and other ailments that caused her doctor to tell her she must go on a stringent reducing diet. However, he did not recommend what kind of diet.

As Mrs. B. was one of my lecture members, she asked my advice and I gave her the complete Oriental diet system. The first two days, after fasting, she found she had lost four pounds. This, of course, was mostly water. But it encouraged her. When she began the actual reducing diet she suffered no hardships, for she found she did not miss the cakes, starches, sugars and carbohydrates she had taken daily for some years. The rice gave her a comfortably full feeling. The dieting soup satisfied her hunger pangs between meals, and in the first week of her diet she shed 14 pounds. This was so encouraging that she was able to easily extend her diet to another 7-day period. In this week she got rid of 20 more pounds. She kept the diet up for two more weeks, and easily lost the other 14 pounds and was down to her normal weight of 130 pounds. She was able to wear some of her former dresses, and the doctor told her when he examined her that her blood pressure was now normal and her heart action was improved over the time when she weighed 185 pounds. But the greatest benefits came in her relationships with her family and her husband. She now had the vitality and energy to enjoy her life and to do her normal work without fatigue and boredom.

You can actually follow this Oriental reducing plan for several weeks and not be undernourished or suffer from hunger pangs, until you have lost your desired weight. Then, if you should start to overeat again, and get back five or ten pounds, you can go back immediately on the 7-day diet until you are back to normal weight once more.

Later in this book, you will be given many delicious recipes for preparing vegetables Oriental style, which will give you a wide variety of different dishes to serve with your meals, not only while you are losing weight pleasantly but when you go on the sustaining diet and wish to keep your weight at a fixed level.

You will also not be denied desserts, for I shall give you many fascinating Oriental desserts, utilizing the natural fruits that can give your sweet tooth a chance to be satisfied without taking into your body dangerous white sugars, white denatured flour and the starches which we find in most American desserts and which are quickly turned into stored fat by the body!

— 3 —

Eat for Enjoyment
as Well as for Health

Eating should be enjoyable and not just for purposes of maintaining the body in good health. In any form of dieting many people lose sight of this fact. They go into various diets with a do-or-die determination that often robs them of one of life's greatest joys.

When you have attained the desired weight through my Oriental miracle diet, you face the problem of maintaining that weight and yet, at the same time, enjoying your food and not feeling that you are a slave to a system that keeps you slender but deprives you of one of life's greatest pleasures—eating.

There are many variations to this diet and many foods that you can continue to take on your sustaining diet, which will not only keep the pounds from ever coming back, but will give you adequate nourishment and at the same time supply your taste buds with a pleasureable sensation that makes you feel you are really enjoying your food.

In this chapter we shall investigate some of these foods that may be eaten to vary the Oriental diet and which you will also require to keep the pounds off on your sustaining diet.

THE DIFFERENCE BETWEEN CARBOHYDRATE FOODS AND PROTEIN FOODS

There is one important difference between carbohydrate foods and protein foods—it is chiefly one of taste. Carbohydrates are enjoyable to your taste buds because they are sweet. But the carbohydrates are dangerous if overused, because they quickly are converted into fat. The trick in any sustaining diet, after you have lost the desired number of pounds, is to substitute high protein foods for the carbohydrates that you formerly ate and which brought back your weight quickly after dieting.

These high protein foods not only give you better nutrition but they also give pleasure to your taste buds. They also tend to give you a feeling of being well fed, controlling your hunger thermostat which makes you constantly crave sugars, starches and carbohydrates. On these high protein sustaining foods your body will actually be better nourished and the extra pounds which you worked hard to get rid of, will not come back quickly.

You may still maintain a brown rice diet but now, after losing the desired pounds, if you wish to retain your present desirable weight, eat the following foods, with the addition of the reducing vegetables given elsewhere.

A normal portion of these meats may be eaten, always broiled, boiled or fried without fat in a teflon pan:

Ground beef with all fat removed.
Steaks, with fat trimmed off.
Chicken, broiled or baked, with skin removed.
Turkey, also with skin removed.
Leg of lamb baked.
Veal.

In addition to the above meats, which furnish the body with adequate protein, you should also vary the diet by including in your sustaining diet some of the following organ meats. Not only are these economical but they contain valuable nutrients often not found in more expensive cuts of meat.

Beef or calf's liver. (Calf's liver is more expensive and yet not more nutritional than the cheaper beef liver.)

Kidneys.

Hearts.

Brains. (These may be added to scrambled eggs and make an excellent breakfast or luncheon dish. A little margarine may be used to cook them in.)

Sweetbreads.

During your actual 7-day reducing period avoid all pork products, but these may be added in small quantities after the desired weight has been lost. You can then eat bacon, which has been thoroughly cooked, removing most of the fat. It must be remembered, in eating any form of pork, that it is higher in caloric content than other meats. For instance, there are three times more calories in one-half pound of pork sausage than there are in one-half pound of round steak. If you eat pork products, even on your sustaining diet, you face a risk of increasing your calories to a level that may bring back the pounds you have lost in dieting.

Also on the prohibited list while you are on your 7-day reducing diet are such foods as frankfurters, knockwurst, liverwurst and other processed meats. After you have lost the desired weight you may eat small portions of these products without fear.

You may eat fish during the diet period and after. Fish is one of the finest forms of protein and has an advantage over meat in that it has less fat.

Shrimps, lobster, crab, canned tuna and canned salmon may be added to your diet for variety, while you are on the 7-day Oriental diet. Then, when you are on your sustaining diet, you may use fish, and increase the portions. The fish can be eaten with vegetables, brown rice, or by itself.

Shrimp, crab and lobster may be added to tasty cold salads, with a nonfattening dressing (to be given later). Or you may bake or broil other forms of fish. You should avoid fried fish, even on the sustaining diet, for it becomes saturated with fat and this adds to the calories. After all, a total, daily caloric intake of 2,500 for women, and about 3,200 for men, is required to keep the body at its normal weight and any intake beyond these limits is bound to bring the fat back quickly. Although, we do not worry about calories while on the reducing 7-day Oriental diet because you can hardly eat more than 1,000 calories a day no matter how much you eat of the reducing soup, the vegetables and proteins given in this diet. We shall later have something to say about when calories do count in maintaining a normal weight and it becomes vitally important to know about the effects of exercise and the caloric requirements for various types of workers and those who lead sedentary lives with little physical activity.

You may also eat every type of cheese in small portions during dieting and afterwards on your sustaining diet to maintain you at normal weight. Dairy products are also helpful in obtaining your required daily amounts of protein, and this includes cottage cheese, pot cheese, yogurt and processed cheeses. You may drink skimmed milk, two glasses a day, and also use it in cooking various desserts, including rice pudding and custard. Eggs make a good variation to meat protein intake and later, I shall give you some delicious recipes, which can make eggs more tasteful and nourishing than the usual frying, poaching or boiling.

The above-mentioned protein foods are valuable in any diet plan, for they give you that variety which makes you feel you are eating all you wish and yet, with the sure knowledge that these foods will give you a balanced diet and will keep the unwanted pounds off in the future.

After you have lost your desired pounds you have to be eternally vigilant that you do not allow yourself to become careless in your sustaining diet and eat an excess of fat-producing carbohydrate foods, as the following case from my files illustrates.

Louise L. was a young school teacher whose weight was 155 pounds when she started the 7-day Oriental diet. She wanted to lose 25 pounds to be back to her normal 130 pounds. She began the diet and it took her three weeks to lose the excess poundage for she did not follow the diet too rigidly. But after the three weeks she was delighted that she no longer had to watch her weight so carefully so she began to go back to her former diet. Soon the scales were tipping dangerously in the vicinity of 140 pounds. Louise then realized it was time to do something drastic. It was at this time that she consulted me.

I found out that Louise was making the old mistakes that had kept the fat on her body before. She was eating about 2,700 calories a day, but they were mostly fat-producing foods, high in carbohydrates. Here was her typical diet:

For breakfast she ate a dish of popular brand cereal with milk and sugar. She had two cups of coffee, with cream and sugar. She also had a glass of orange juice and two slices of white toast with real butter.

Louise ate lunch near her school and it usually consisted of a piece of fried or broiled meat; sometimes, it was a hamburger, with cheese and on a white bun. She varied this luncheon at times with macaroni, and occasionally, with her hamburger she had french fried potatoes and topped it off with a malt, or a piece of pie or cake, and with another cup of coffee with cream and sugar!

You can well understand why Louise was soon right back where she started on this vicious cycle of overindulgence of fattening foods. To make matters worse, at dinner she ate another meat dish, with vegetables flavored with real butter, and again a carbohydrate dessert of ice cream, jello, cake, or something equally fattening, and with another cup of coffee and cream.

On this diet Louise was eating more than 3,000 calories a day and these were fat calories—that is, fat-producing foods. She actually only needed about 2,000 calories a day for her work schedule for she did little physical work. During the reducing diet with the Oriental system, she had actually consumed less than 1,200 calories a day, and that was one of the reasons why her weight loss was gradual.

The moment that Louise discovered her weight was coming back rapidly she became most discouraged. When she consulted me I told her that even on her sustaining diet she must eat fewer carbohydrates and proteins than she was taking. In fact, she had to keep her daily caloric intake to about 2,000 calories a day or the weight would come back rapidly.

Louise began a sustaining diet which included the following foods. For breakfast:

Two boiled eggs.
A small orange juice or half a grapefruit.
Two slices of bacon with all fat cooked out.
One slice of whole-wheat bread with margarine.
Coffee with a non-dairy, non-fat milk and artificial sugar.

For lunch Louise could still have a portion of lean meat and it could be veal, beef or chicken, broiled or cooked without fat. She could eat no more than two of the vegetables that grow above ground, such as corn, or peas, which are not listed on the 7-day diet group of vegetables. She could vary this with any other vegetables she wished on other days. No bread or butter was permitted at lunch, but she could eat a bowlful of brown rice flavored with margarine, and have a glass of skimmed milk, with sugarless jello or fruit for dessert.

Now, you can well see that this was no starvation diet for Louise. Yet it was a sustaining diet that could keep her slender and at the same time furnish her with a balanced, nutritional diet. For dinner I told Louise to eat a small bowl of the diet soup, to kill her appetite. This gave her bulk. Then she could eat a regular portion of ground beef, with fat removed and broiled, or fried without fat. Or she could vary this on some nights with a small steak, broiled; a small salad, with lemon and oil dressing, and if she was still hungry, (which was unlikely if she ate the vegetable soup) she could add one or two vegetables such as broccoli or asparagus tips, with a little melted butter. For dessert she could have a portion of fresh fruit or canned fruit if the syrup was all washed off.

The upshot of this new sustaining diet was that Louise was back to her normal 130 pounds within two weeks. From that time she simply maintained her regular sustaining diet, adding proteins instead of carbohydrates to her daily food intake, until she found the perfect diet to keep her at ner desired weight.

THE DANGER OF SKIPPING BREAKFAST FOR WEIGHT REDUCTION

Many people advocate skipping breakfast entirely while trying to lose weight, believing that the few calories they save in this way can then be added to lunch or dinner. This is a fallacy. Going without breakfast can often be dangerous for it often leads to severe hunger that causes one to overeat at lunch and dinner, wiping out all the benefits gained by going without breakfast.

Most nutritional experts agree that doing without breakfast is a poor way to lose weight. The body needs food in the morning to build the blood sugar level, which may have dropped dangerously low overnight. If you do without breakfast, or eat only coffee and orange juice in the mistaken notion you are reducing your caloric intake, you may feel early morning reactions such as fatigue, irritability, weakness in the knees, dizziness, faintness, blurred vision or other typical symptoms.

When breakfast-skippers feel such symptoms they usually take some carbohydrate food, thinking they are raising their blood sugar content. Actually they are lowering it. Here is why: When carbohydrates are taken into the body insulin is released to help the liver store the sugar. The sugar is changed into a substance known as glycogen and the body is still deprived of the energy it needs after sleeping eight hours without any form of nourishment.

When you eat a good solid protein breakfast of eggs, bacon, cheese, or an omelet using eggs and cheese, or other foods such as onions, mushrooms, chicken livers, or jelly, you not only build the blood sugar level quickly but you will also have steady energy until lunch time and not feel hungry, irritable and weak.

VARIETY OF BREAKFAST DISHES
POSSIBLE ON SUSTAINING DIET

If you become bored with eggs on a reducing diet or on the sustaining diet, and you do not like them plain boiled or fried, try combining them either in omelets, or with meat products, such as kidneys, sausage, Canadian bacon, ham or cheese. A very tasty omelet can be made with a combination of fried onions and Philadelphia cream cheese. You may also use Cheddar cheese and onions, with eggs, to prepare a tasty omelet. Kippered herrings in an omelet is also found to be a tasty variation if you are bored with the usual egg dishes.

HOW A TRUCK DRIVER KEPT DOWN HIS WEIGHT

Truck drivers are notoriously heavyweights. This is due to the fact they stop frequently at roadside cafes and eat the invariable pie, cake or doughnuts with coffee and cream and sugar. They have little exercise, and soon the bulging hips and abdomen show the results of their overindulgence in carbohydrate foods.

Jerry B. was such a truck driver, who sought me out when his weight had increased to 225 pounds. He wanted to lose weight but he was afraid that he would not have sufficient strength to stay alert and active on his driving job.

He wanted to reduce down to his normal weight of about 185 pounds. I estimated that Jerry was eating about 4,000 calories a day and I told him that the body could hardly lose weight until the caloric intake was cut to about 1,000 a day. He groaned at this, as he visualized himself practically starving to death!

Then when I told him that he could eat several times a day, on my Oriental diet, and never feel fatigue or hunger, a sigh of relief escaped him and he was ready to listen.

I gave Jerry the basic brown rice and vegetable soup diet, with instructions to carry a thermos jug of the soup along with him in the cab of his truck. He was to eat a generous bowl of soup whenever he felt hungry. In another container, I told him to carry brown rice, already cooked and mixed with margarine. It stayed warm in the thermos jug he carried. He ate lunch out but returned to his home for dinner, as he drove only between two cities, which permitted him to live at his home. He was put on a substantial breakfast of two eggs, any style, one piece of whole-wheat toast with butter, coffee with cream and sugar, and with his two eggs he could have some form of meat—bacon, sausage or ham, and on occasion, a lean, small steak. For dinner he was to eat only a bowl of rice, with two vegetables, and a steak, or patty of ground lean meat, with fruit or jello for dessert. Jerry's weight did not melt away rapidly, for this would have been unwise in his heavy work.

Jerry lost only about five pounds every week but within several months he had lost 40 pounds without in any way feeling he was dieting and without loss of energy or endangering his health.

After Jerry had lost his desired pounds he went on the sustaining diet, using the basic rice and vegetables and eating any lean meat he wanted twice a day, with his usual heavy breakfast. Jerry checked regularly with me for some time and he never had a weight problem again. He cut out all starches, sugars and other heavy carbohydrate foods, substituting in their place the heavy protein foods such as eggs, cheese and meats.

When Jerry stopped for a coffee break at roadside cafes, or to have his lunch, he did not eat the usual cake, pie, doughnuts or ice cream; instead he would eat a chicken salad, no bread, and for dessert, some fruit or jello and occasionally rice pudding or custard. Sometimes he would vary this with a green salad, or a tuna salad, a small steak, and two nonfattening vegetables. Jerry stayed at his desired weight simply by cutting down on general food intake and avoiding sugars, starches, creamy desserts and cream in his coffee. He learned to drink his coffee black and with artificial sugar instead of regular white sugar. This last item was important to Jerry, as he stopped on the road and often drank as many as five or six cups of coffee a day.

IF YOU MUST EAT SANDWICHES _____ !

The American habit of eating sandwiches with thick slices of white bread for lunch, and hamburgers on buns for dinner, can often add those extra calories which add up to excess fat being stored in the body.

If you eat just two slices of white bread a day for one year, without regard to limiting other calories, you can add as much as 30 pounds a year to your weight! This is why the weight sneaks back so insidiously on most people who stop dieting and go back to the old eating habits that put the weight on in the first place.

If you must eat sandwiches and feel lost without them, why not try protein sandwiches? Fold a hamburger between two slices of Cheddar cheese and you will have a delicious protein substitute for the white bread normally used to make a sandwich. Or use two slices of baloney to fold various types of cheese into. You can eat hamburger patties with slices of onion, cheese or bacon strips, and never miss the extra bread that most Americans seem to require with their ground meat.

Another delicious sandwich can be made with Philadelphia cream cheese spread on slices of baloney, then folded over like a sandwich. You can also use slices of yellow cheese; chop up ground meat, onions and mushrooms and spread them on the slices of cheese. These are pure protein and can be added to any reducing diet to give flavor and variety to meals.

If the sandwich habit is too deeply ingrained to break all at once, start by eliminating one slice of bread and have an open-faced sandwich of hamburger or cheese, with a slice of onion, relish, mustard or anything else you desire on it. Then as you accustom yourself to the one slice of bread you can gradually eliminate that until you are satisfied with the protein foods that you can fix to appear like tasty sandwiches.

Many people who are on this Oriental diet and do not want to give up bread have reported good results with the protein breads that are on the market. But try to keep even these breads down to two slices a day while on the reducing diet. Then, when on the sustaining diet, you should eliminate bread from most meals, eating one or two pieces of whole-wheat toast for breakfast.

IN-BETWEEN SNACKS HELP KEEP YOU ON YOUR DIET

Even on the Oriental 7-day diet, which gives you as much as four pounds of food a day, including the vegetable soup, you may occasionally feel that you would like to snack between meals, but you are at a loss as to what you should eat.

You can add variety to the Oriental diet by substituting other foods to those already given. You can have a tasty nibble of chicken salad, cold shrimp, or lobster tail. You can also eat two frankfurters or munch on a variety of cheeses between meals. You can even have a slice of steak or half a can of tuna or salmon.

As long as you stick with the protein foods you will not be eating the fat-producing foods and you will notice that you do not put on those extra pounds you would if you ate sandwiches with bread, and added cakes, pies, ice creams or other forms of carbohydrates. This simple secret will keep you from being excessively hungry all day and you can even eat three or four walnuts, almonds or Brazil nuts between meals and you will not add weight. Too many nuts, however, being rich in oils, can build up excess fat, so eat them sparingly.

ZSA-ZSA GABOR REVEALED
HER SLENDERIZING SECRETS

Years ago, when Zsa-Zsa Gabor was married to Conrad Hilton, the famous hotel man, she was at my home in Bel-Air at a big party honoring Lady Thelma Furness and her twin sister, Gloria Vanderbilt.

Everyone marvelled at the beautifully proportioned, slender figure of Zsa-Zsa, and over the lavish dinner, served in a huge tent on the sumptuous lawn of the estate, I observed that she did not eat all the rich foods served to the guests. We had fruit cup made of fresh fruits, to start, and this was followed with small salads made of asparagus tips and grapefruit segments, with a tasty French dressing. The meat course was filet mignon, with rissole potatoes, and dessert was fresh melon balls, drenched in grenadine. I noticed that Zsa-Zsa ate small portions of the food, and did not touch the rich appetizers that were served to the guests with their drinks, before the dinner.

Recently, at a big party in Beverly Hills, I had a chance to talk to the still glamorous, still slender Zsa-Zsa, who is even more youthful and lovelier than ever, and I found out that she is well versed in the dietetic sciences. She still prefers salads to heavy, rich carbohydrates and too much meat. She still eats vegetables, preferably raw and in salads, and I noticed that she did not touch the lavish, frosted birthday cake being served, but chose pieces of fresh fruit from the enormous fruit bowl that served as an attractive centerpiece. She seldom ever eats cakes, pies, ice cream or other carbohydrates, but sticks to fruits for her sources of sugars and carbohydrates.

WHAT LOW-CALORIE DESSERTS CAN YOU EAT?

Because most people have such a sweet tooth, from their habit of eating so many carbohydrates, it is impossible for them to ever conceive of reducing without having some form of dessert.

The following desserts are low in carbohydrates and can be eaten in small quantities, while on the Oriental 7-day reducing diet. The average serving of about one-half cup will average only about 60 calories per portion.

Apples, baked or stewed, with a little artificial sweetening. Or the apples may be eaten raw.
Jello.
Cherries.
Grapefruit, with artificial sweetener, if you like it sweet.

Banana custard or similar desserts with butterscotch junkets or chocolate (without sugar, these are now on the market and have an
average of only 40 calories per portion).

Banana with skimmed milk.

Raspberries or blueberries with milk.

Watermelon.

Cantaloupe or honeydew melon.

Peaches.

Pineapple (fresh, unless you eat the canned pineapple that is cooked in
its natural juices, without sugar).

You can add a wide variety of fruits to the above list. Also,
you can check my list of Oriental desserts which I shall give later,
to find those that please you. Remember, sugar should not be used
during the period of losing weight, as each teaspoonful is about 15
calories. Try to find some artificial sugar that pleases you. There
are several excellent brands on the market.

THE FORBIDDEN FOODS IN THE
ORIENTAL REDUCING DIET

While you are on the rather strict Oriental 7-day diet, even if
it is continued to three or four periods, it is important that you
avoid the following forbidden foods. When you have lost the
desired pounds you can add some of these forbidden foods but
remember, they will always quickly add to your weight and should
be carefully watched or avoided entirely.

Mashed potatoes and gravy.

Potatoes, fried or boiled. (Although a baked potato with margarine can
sometimes be eaten to add variety.)

All desserts made with sugars, including canned fruits in heavy syrups.
(If these are used sparingly, wash away the syrup carefully.)

Ice cream, cakes and pies made with sugar. (Instead of these, substitute
cheese, fresh fruits, or make the above desserts with artificial
sugar.)

Also on the forbidden list, while reducing, are all gravies made with
white flour, and mayonnaise and salad dressings heavy with oil.

Beer, wines and cocktails of all kinds are to be rigidly avoided if you are
serious about losing weight.

TO GIVE YOUR TASTE BUDS AN EXTRA
BOOST DO THE FOLLOWING:

Use soybean sauce with a touch of Worcester sauce added to pep up your rice, vegetables or other foods.

When cooking dietetic foods add a touch of sherry wine to the sauce. (This is not enough to do any harm to your diet.)

To make a good salad dressing that will be low in calories, mix a little mayonnaise with ketchup and add a touch of plain apple cider vinegar. Despite the fact that mayonnaise is high in calories, a small amount on salads will add interest to your foods and you can cut down on some other high-caloric food when you use this dressing.

If you are at home a good deal during this 7-day Oriental diet, keep protein foods in your refrigerator that you can eat when you are hungry. Some of these can be left-over meats, chicken, hamburger, chicken livers, leg of lamb or other meats that were left over from the previous night's dinner.

Slices of baloney, cheeses, yogurt and even cold shrimps can be eaten between meals in small quantities. But best of all, if hunger pangs assail you between meals, eat a heaping bowl of the vegetable soup with some Parmesan cheese sprinkled on top and it will help kill your appetite for hours and give you that full feeling which makes you feel you have just eaten a big meal.

Dieting should never become boring and monotonous. You can add variety to your reducing diet and also to the sustaining diet that you will use to keep your weight at a normal level after shedding the unwanted pounds.

— 4 —

Some Facts You Should Know About Reducing Foods and Fattening Foods

In continuing the Oriental diet for reducing without hunger, it is important that you know the truth about what are reducing foods and what are fattening foods.

This information is vitally important if you are going to embark on a reducing diet that extends beyond the 7-day period and if you want to lose from 20 to 100 pounds. In fact, this information is important also when you go on the sustaining diet to keep your weight at normal, so you will not have that perpetual struggle that plagues all dieters—a quick return of the unwanted ugly fat!

When you have taken off the desired weight there will be a continual struggle all your life to keep that weight off. If you continue on the basic Oreintal diet and avoid making the mistakes so many people make, you can go on to a healthier, happier life and still enjoy the foods you eat without the feelings of frustration which often beset people who think they must keep on a rigid diet the rest of their lives.

GIRL WHO IGNORED BASIC FOOD RULES
GAINED BACK LOST WEIGHT

Gladys R. weighed 150 pounds when she came to me for help. She could not stop eating fattening foods like spaghetti, mashed potatoes with gravy, creamy, rich desserts, and candies. She was given the diet regimen in Chapter 2 and it worked beautifully for her. The rice, being highly satisfying to her carbohydrate-trained taste buds, gave her great satisfaction so long as she continued eating it with the other basic diet foods. She felt satisfied and her craving for sweets ended.

This is one of the most important things to remember in your sustaining diet: you must continue to eat some carbohydrate foods each day, but not in excess of 200 calories, otherwise the body can easily suffer from a condition known as acidosis.

Many people who eat excessive quantities of meat, or other forms of proteins, can also take on this condition. So Gladys was happy on her Oriental diet and kept at it until she had lost 30 pounds. Then she was at her normal weight for her height and age.

Soon, however, she began to add more carbohydrates to her diet. At noon she would sneak in a malted milk. She ate one sandwich at lunch. She ate toast, butter and marmalade for breakfast. She drank her coffee with cream and sugar and soon she had put on 20 of the 30 pounds she had lost on her oriental diet. Then she became really alarmed and realized that the battle against fat was a lifetime one and that she simply could not ignore basic facts about fattening and reducing foods.

It was then that I put Gladys back on the stringent Oriental diet until she was once again back to her normal weight. Then I put her on a sustaining diet which included brown rice three times a week, vegetables, meat and fruits. She could not binge on ice cream or malted milks often, and if she did, she had to diet for two extra days to catch up. Soon Gladys reported she no longer had the craving for sweets and starches she once had and she was holding the line at her desired weight.

IMPORTANT TO KNOW WHEN CALORIES DO COUNT

In the battle among nutritionists as to whether one should bother with calories or ignore them, both sides are really right, to a certain extent. In my Oriental 7-day reducing diet I do not advise you to count calories for you can hardly eat more than 1,000 calories on the reducing soup, rice and other limited foods given in the diet. However, you should know which foods, including meats and carbohydrates, are the highest in calories and then avoid those that are extremely high and favor those that are low in calories. In this way, you can add variety to your reducing diet and also keep yourself on the low-calorie foods when you go on the sustaining diet to maintain your normal body weight.

Following are the low-calorie meats which you may select from, in the Oriental system of dieting, to go with the brown rice and vegetable soup. The following calories are given for a serving of about ¼ pound of meat or 4 ounces.

	Calories
Ground meat, with fat trimmed off	215
Boiled or broiled beef	250
Chuck steak, trimmed without fat	275
Sirloin steak	195
Filet mignon	210
Pot roast	200
T-bone steak	210
Beef hearts	135
Beef or lamb kidneys	225
Beef or calf's liver	165
Sweetbreads	205
Tenderloin steak	240
Lamb (with fat trimmed off)	200
Lamb chops (broiled)	165
Lamb kidneys	115

The following fish can be utilized for protein in place of meat and it will readily be seen that fish is much lower in calories than most cuts of meat.

Fish in low-calorie list:	Calories
Shrimps	125
Tuna (fresh or canned)	190
Sea bass	105
Raw oysters	60
Salmon	135
Flounder	80
Cod steaks	100
Abalone	120
Shad roe	175

Dairy products in low-calorie list:	Calories
Cottage cheese	135
Buttermilk	80
Skimmed milk	50
Evaporated milk	185
Yogurt	85
Whole milk	90

Poultry in low calorie list:	Calories
Turkey (not stuffed)	200
Broiled chicken	165
Roasted chicken	215

From these lists you may select a variety of low-calorie foods to vary any reducing plan. This may be necessary if you extend the Oriental 7-day diet to two or more weeks, and you desire losing from 20 to 50 more pounds. Then you can eat any of the protein foods in the low-calorie lists. However, remember, that these low-calorie foods can also add weight if large quantities are eaten. That is why I give you the calories for an average serving of ¼ pound of meat a day. If you are trying to lose weight with the Oriental system, or any system, and you eat large quantities of even these low-calorie foods daily and the calories exceed 1,000 a day, you will hold your own *but you will definitely not lose weight!*

Then there are high-calorie foods which you should avoid while you are on the 7-day Oriental diet plan, and also when you are on your sustaining diet. Remember, these high-calorie foods add up more quickly on the calorie list and should be used cautiously and only small portions consumed. *They should be completely eliminated while you are on the 7-day Oriental reducing diet.*

List of high calorie foods to avoid while on 7-day Oriental diet (based on 4 oz. serving):

	Calories
Frankfurters	305
Swiss steak	400
Hamburger	390
Tongue	340
Cube steak	345
Porterhouse steak	390
Rib roast	325
Poultry:	
Chicken croquettes	370
Roast, stuffed turkey	490
Chicken with dumplings	540
Roast stuffed chicken	340

Dairy products high in calories to avoid while dieting (calories for 4 ounces of weight):

	Calories
Cream	410
Butter	920
Milk (condensed, sweet)	395
Malted milk	510

Fish products that are high in calories to avoid during 7-day Oriental diet:

	Calories
Fried shrimp	265
Canned Salmon	250
Mackerel	295

Oysters, fried	275
Sardines in oil	375
Codfish cakes	245

Calories contained by alcoholic beverages, to be avoided during 7-day Oriental diet (calories per 4 liquid ounces):

	Calories
Beer	65
Ale	70
Rum	390
Cognac	240
Gin	310
Champagne	125
Brandy	240
Sherry	140
Whiskey	400
Vermouth, dry	240
Vermouth, sweet	240
Vodka	310
Dry wine	80
Sweet wine	135

Avoid the following foods while on your 7-day reducing plan, as they are high in calories and are to be avoided. They can be eaten moderately after you have lost your desired weight, but they should be used sparingly at all times if you wish to avoid putting the unwanted pounds back on again.

Cakes	Dressings for salads	Hominy
Cookies	Fried eggs	Grits
Candies	Ice cream	Fatty soups
Corn starch puddings	Mayonnaise	Sugar
Jellies and marmalades	Fatty meats	Oils of all kinds
Crackers	Pancakes	Syrups
Sundaes, malts	Sodas	Waffles
Corn meal	Popcorn	

USEFUL POINTERS ON PREPARING
LOW-CALORIE MEATS

In using the 7-day Oriental food plan to lose weight, you will naturally stick to the daily intake of brown rice, and the vegetables, prepared in the greaseless soup, which has all the reducing vegetables in it.

However, to satisfy your body's needs for proteins, even while you are dieting, you will require some of the low-calorie meats to give balance to your diet. It is important that you know how to prepare these so as to avoid excess fats.

Of course you realize that no meat is actually free of fat or fat calories. While on the reducing diet for the first seven days, you can have a small portion of meat each day with the rice and vegetables. However, meat should not be fried, but broiled. Meats that are fried absorb the fats and oils and increase the caloric intake nearly 100 percent.

If you cook with the modern Teflon cookware you may be able to get away with frying hamburgers, if you use only chuck ground meat, which contains less fat than the regular ground beef.

If you fry the ground chuck it will lose most of its fat. No matter how lean meat is ground it always contains some veins of fat but this will usually fry out in the pan and can be drained off.

The best way to prepare your meats, fish, chicken or lamb, to obtain the highest benefits for a reducing regime, is to broil them. This helps remove most of the fats, as the fat drops into the bottom of the drip pan and does not become involved with the meat, as it does in the frying process.

You can also roast the low-calorie meats that you use in the 7-day Oriental diet plan, but be especially careful when roasting meats, chicken or fish *not* to baste these. You can pour a little water over them if they should be too dry in cooking.

The Oriental diet plan suggests using more fish than other forms of protein. Substitute fish as often as possible while you are reducing, for fish is an excellent form of protein and has fewer calories than meat.

Many nutritional experts now believe that fish is a superior form of protein to meat. They ascribe the health of the Japanese people, and their high vitality and energy, to the fact that fish is high on their list of protein foods. As Japan is primarily not an agricultural country, they subsist mostly on our Oriental reducing diet products of rice, vegetables, fruits and fish. They seldom eat red-blooded meats such as beef, and limited amounts of pork.

These people are usually thin, wiry, energetic, and suffer less from high blood pressure, arthritis, heart trouble and other diseases which afflict the predominantly meat-eating nations of the world.

The Chinese people subsist mainly on this same diet, which I advocate for weight reduction, of rice, fish and vegetables. Of course, both peoples eat many grains, such as rice, wheat, oats, barley and soy beans, which are high in protein value. They stay slender and suffer from few of our modern American diseases.

Many East Indians, Tibetans and those living in Hunza, have lived to be from 110 to 135 years of age. I have investigated their diets and have found that they subsisted primarily on grains, vegetables, fruits, nuts, cheese and milk products, such as yogurt and cottage cheese and whey, which is the watery liquid that gathers on the top of milk when it is allowed to stand and ferment. The Hunzas, who seem to be especially healthy and slender as well as long-lived, claim many of their health benefits derive from the apricot, which they dry for use in winter, and eat all year round. They claim special virtues for this golden fruit, and even believe that it gives them long life and better health. The Hunzas seldom eat red-blooded meats, subsisting entirely on a diet that would be considered inadequate in America, of fruits, nuts, grains, vegetables and dairy products.

Man I Met In India 120 Years Old Used This Diet

I once met a man in my travels to India who was 120 years of age and he gave me his diet, which I found was, in many ways, similar to the one we are using in our Oriental 7-day reducing diet. He was like a man of 50 or 60. He had perfect eyesight, he had his own teeth, a fine head of hair, and a sharp, clear mind.

I visited his home on the outskirts of Calcutta and there he showed me his vegetable garden, where he had several different types of vegetables growing. He had two goats, which he milked and from this he obtained much of his protein.

This man ate whenever he felt hungry. He munched on some nuts or fruits several times a day. His main diet was a bowl of natural rice, goat's milk and steamed vegetables, although he told me that he tried to eat most of his fresh vegetables raw. He had goat's cheese, occasionally an egg, and for desserts he had figs, dates, melons, and other fruits in season. The bread he served me was heavy and coarse, and he told me it was made from stone-ground wheat and barley, with goat's milk and wild honey. He told me he had not eaten meat for over 75 years, and once in a while he ate broiled fish, when some neighbor made him a special gift of fresh fish caught in a nearby stream.

This healthy Indian told me that he had tried eating red-blooded meat 75 years ago and found that it gave him such unpleasant symptoms that he stopped after a few weeks. When he stopped eating meat his condition improved at once, and he never again touched this form of protein.

He also told me that he occasionally ate lentils, and also beans. He showed me how he prepared these with onions, tomato sauce, a half cup of vegetable oil, and a little salt. He let these simmer on the stove for one or two hours, until tender, and these seemed to satisfy his protein needs. I do not recommend the bean and lentil family as foods while you are on this 7-day reducing plan, but they may occasionally be used as good sources of protein when you are on the sustaining diet, after having lost your desired weight.

For desserts he was fond of yogurt, which he made himself from goat's milk. He put a little natural wild honey on this for flavor, but honey is not recommended while on your 7-day diet to lose weight, for it is a very high form of carbohydrate. It can sometimes be used for flavoring. But when you are on your sustaining diet you can use honey instead of sugar, if you wish. He also ate dates, figs, dried apricots and prunes, as well as all fruits in season. I was astonished to find that he rarely had orange juice, but he did get his Vitamin C from other foods, particularly melons, when they were in season. He also had taken a whole lemon in a glass of water, upon arising, for many years.

HOW TO USE DAIRY PRODUCTS
WHILE ON THIS REDUCING DIET

While you are on the 7-day Oriental reducing diet you can use dairy products in moderation. After you have lost the desired weight you can increase your intake of these excellent proteins from milk products.

Milk

Milk can be taken whole, either pasteurized or raw. Many nutrition experts agree that the raw, unpasteurized milk is far superior to that which has been boiled. The raw milk is supervised and free of disease and contains many elements that the pasteurized milk does not contain.

Children fed on a diet of raw milk were found to be healthier and to have fewer dietetic problems than those who drank pasteurized milk. Anything boiled, such as pasteurized milk, is changed in its chemistry and is no longer as valuable as a food for human beings.

Skimmed milk should be substituted for raw whole milk if you wish to avoid the fat content of whole milk during your 7-day period of reducing. When you are on your regular sustaining diet, you may take as much as two glasses of whole milk daily, if you are over 20 years of age, and at least three to four glasses if under 20 (while the bones and teeth are maturing).

In considering whether you should or should not drink whole milk, realize that your body, even during periods of dieting, requires some fat to help the metabolic processes. At least two tablespoonfuls of some form of fat are permissible, even while reducing. Also remember, it is not fat that makes fat in the body, but the carbohydrates, sugars, starches and certain forms of oil, such as olive oil and some animal fats.

Avoid all evaporated, canned milk, or condensed milk, with sugar, during this period of dieting. These are extremely high in calories and should be avoided in any weight-reducing regime.

What about cream, butter, cottage cheese and other dairy products?

A small amount of real cream may be taken in your breakfast coffee, even when reducing, as you do need some fat in your diet. Sugar can be eliminated in favor of some sugar substitute, as the sugar has calories that are converted into fat very easily. If you want to cut down on the cream in your coffee you may take a non-dairy cream substitute.

Butter should be avoided during this 7-day reducing diet and a tablespoonful of margarine should be used on your whole-wheat bread or toast. For salads, avoid olive oil while you are dieting because olive oil increases the caloric intake, and you can substitute corn oil, which is lower in calories and unsaturated fats. Fat that comes into the body from eating too much olive oil remains in the body longer and is most difficult to remove. This is one reason why many people in Latin countries who use excessive amounts of olive oil become very heavy as they advance in age and seldom ever lose the fat they have accumulated over years of eating olive oil.

Cheese and Cheese Products

Most cheeses and cheese products are full of salt and other preservatives and should not be eaten in excessive amounts during a diet for losing weight. If less lean meat is eaten however, some cheese may be substituted and cottage cheese may be eaten as it is lower in calories than other cheeses.

Eggs

You can eat some eggs in moderation while on this Oriental reducing diet but they should not be fried. They should be poached or boiled. When you fry eggs or put cream into scrambled or shirred eggs, the calorie count almost doubles.

HOW MUCH WATER SHOULD YOU DRINK DAILY WHILE DIETING?

Water intake should be slightly increased during this 7-day reducing period, for this reason: Body fat is burned up more quickly and carried from the system if at least 8 glasses of water are drunk each day. While on this 7-day reducing diet avoid drinking ice cold water or soft drinks. The effect on the stomach is very severe when you drink ice cold beverages. Cold water without ice is preferable.

Some reducing systems insist on drinking all the water that can be taken daily, but this is not essential in our Oriental system of dieting. Drink when thirsty, and just before going to bed take a full glass of water. Many doctors advise drinking water just before retiring to flush out the kidneys and to avoid the formation of kidney stones. If you awaken in the night and feel thirsty, drink one glass of water. You will find that the average person drinks far too little water, and you will have to be alert while on this reducing diet to drink sufficient amounts of water, at least 8 to 10 glasses daily, to flush out all the excess fats that your body is throwing off.

SHOULD YOU BOTHER COUNTING CALORIES ON THIS DIET?

Although calories do count, you need not bother counting calories in the Oriental diet system. You can hardly eat enough soup and rice to make it worthwhile to count the calories. You will experience such a stuffed feeling on this reducing diet that you cannot possibly eat enough calories to carry you over the danger mark, which would be about 1,200 calories.

In a weight-reducing diet such as this, calories are not important. However, I shall later give you some facts about calories and their importance in your sustaining diet. You will find that if you are a man and eat more than 1,200 calories a day, while on any reducing plan, you will not lose weight. If you are a woman, and eat more than 900 calories, it will be *difficult* if not impossible to lose weight. You may not gain weight, and merely hold your own, but you surely will not lose weight if you eat more than 900 calories daily. For men, the caloric intake should be less than 1,200 for the full week or two that you are on the Oriental system of dieting. You do not need to actually count your calories for this short period of time. If you strictly adhere to this diet you can eat as much as you wish, until hunger is satisfied—you need not suffer from hunger. You will never gain extra pounds on this strict diet and when you have attained your ideal weight, whether it is in one or two or three weeks, you can then be aware of calories and limit your caloric intake, as I shall instruct you in a later chapter dealing with the caloric content of various foods and what your caloric intake should be. This depends on whether you are male or female, and the nature of your work. But more about this later.

— 5 —

Variations to the 7-Day Oriental Reducing Diet

No matter what diet system you follow there are bound to be days when the chosen diet becomes monotonous and your taste buds rebel against the sameness of the foods you eat.

Rather than abandon your Oriental 7-day diet, especially if you have gone into the second or third 7-day period and you are trying to lose from 20 to 50 more pounds, you simply vary the diet, keeping to the same general plan, but with additions to the diet that will in no way keep you from losing weight but will add to the enjoyment of the new foods you will be eating.

THE FIRST DAY VARIATION DIET

Breakfast

1 cup of orange juice, diluted with water
1 egg, boiled or poached
1 slice whole-wheat toast, with margarine
coffee or tea, artificial cream and sweetener

Lunch

1 salmon steak, baked
small fruit salad
1 cup of chicken-rice soup
1 medium tomato
rice pudding

Dinner

baked tuna-cheese Orientale
green beans
small bowl of brown rice with margarine
scoop of orange or lemon sherbet
coffee or tea, with artificial milk and sweetener

Recipe for baked tuna-cheese Orientale, for four people: Saute one onion, chopped fine, in margarine, until golden brown. Add 2 cups skimmed milk until mixture is smooth and thick. Cut up 10 ounces of diced carrots, and add two cans of tuna, 1/4 cup of whole-wheat flour, and 1/2 cup grated Cheddar cheese. Add dietetic salt to flavor; also add black pepper, dab of mustard, and 2 small cans of tomatoes. Put this into a casserole dish and cook in preheated oven of 375 degrees. Top with grated cheese, and bake for short period of time, until cheese has browned slightly.

You can serve this Oriental dish to guests and they need never suspect that you are on a diet!

SECOND DAY VARIATION DIET

Breakfast

glass of orange-pineapple juice
oatmeal with skimmed milk
2 rye or wheat thins
coffee or tea

Lunch

patty of ground round, broiled
1 cup of summer squash
1 cup of asparagus
portion of Jello (made with artificial sugar)
coffee or tea

Dinner

1 cup of reducing soup
5 oz. of lean leg of lamb
1 cup cooked spinach
1 small serving of brown rice
1 cup of banana whip pudding

THIRD DAY VARIATION DIET

Breakfast

1/2 glass of apricot juice or prune juice
creamed tuna on whole-wheat toast or chipped beef on toast (make
    cream sauce with skimmed milk and whole-wheat flour)
coffee or tea

Lunch

1 cup of consommé
1 cup of cole slaw
tuna salad or chicken salad, with low-calorie dressing
two pieces of Zwieback toast with margarine
coffee or tea

Dinner

1 cup of diced cantaloupe
1 bowl of reducing soup
12 large mushrooms, broiled
1 baked potato with margarine
coffee, tea or glass of skimmed milk

FOURTH DAY VARIATION DIET

Breakfast

eggs a la Shanghai (recipe below)
glass of orange juice, diluted
coffee, tea or skimmed milk

Recipe for eggs a la Shanghai (to serve four people):

6 chicken livers cut up fine
2 tsp. margarine
1 small onion cut up fine and cooked in margarine
4 eggs
8 asparagus tips

Saute onions in margarine. Add chicken livers and brown for 5 minutes. Add 1/2 cup water and simmer a few minutes. Scramble eggs in a separate pan that is greased with margarine; cook eggs in pre-heated oven of 375 degrees for five minutes. Then put chicken livers over the eggs, with pieces of asparagus on top. Cook only long enough to firm eggs, and serve.

Lunch

cup of reducing soup
broiled shrimp on bed of brown rice
salad; grapefruit slices on bed lettuce
coffee, tea or skimmed milk

Dinner

cup of reducing soup
Chinese Chow Mein (easy to prepare, see recipe below)

A slight variation to the monotony of lean beef, veal, chicken, and fish is sometimes necessary. In this recipe you will use a bit of diced pork, which adds a few more calories, but as they are fat calories, and your body needs some fat even when reducing, this is permissible if not overdone. (No vegetables are necessary as they are in the Chow Mein.) You will need:

1/2 lb. of pork, diced
3 cups of sliced Chinese cabbage
1 cup of green pepper sliced fine
1 cup of water chestnuts
1 cup of bamboo shoots
1 cup of mushrooms
1 large onion, sliced up
1 clove garlic
1 cup of bean sprouts
4 tablespoons of soy sauce

Saute the pork in a frying pan with little cooking oil; put all the vegetables and other ingredients into the pan and let it simmer over low heat until the vegetables are cooked. Add just enough water to keep it moist while cooking.

Serve on a bed of steamed rice—either white or brown rice will do.

For dessert you may serve fresh fruit of any kind.

FIFTH DAY VARIATION DIET

Breakfast

1/2 glass cranberry juice
two eggs, scrambled in margarine
two pieces of whole-wheat or protein toast
1/2 tsp. jelly on toast
coffee or tea, with cream and artificial sugar

(Do not be afraid to take a little real cream for coffee occasionally, for, remember, even when reducing you need about two tps. of fat a day in the diet. It is generally amply furnished by the meats you eat, but occasionally you can treat yourself to some cream in your coffee without endangering the effectiveness of your reducing diet.)

Lunch

veal cutlet broiled
one cup of reducing vegetable soup
carrot-raisin salad—(Use shredded carrots and 1/2 cup of seedless
        raisins. Soak raisins in water until soft. Serve with a low-calorie
        dressing or a dressing I shall later give for salads.)
fruit, pineapple or peach slices
usual coffee or tea, or glass of skimmed milk or buttermilk

Dinner

Main dish: Sweetbreads on lean piece of ham.

Recipe: 1 lb. of lamb sweetbreads, or beef. Boil for 10 minutes, remove from stove, drain and dry sweetbreads. Melt spoonful of margarine in pan, and add the sweetbreads. Add artificial salt and pepper to taste, and cook only for two minutes. Serve sweetbreads on slice of pre-cooked ham, with two slices of protein or whole-wheat toast. Serve 1/2 baked potato with sour cream with this main dish.

Dessert: lemon or orange or pineapple sherbet.

SIXTH DAY VARIATION DIET

Breakfast

all wheat cereal with skimmed milk
1 spoonful of sugar or a little honey—(Not recommended for regular
    diet menus, but as this is a variation diet, to avoid monotony you
    can indulge yourself on occasion with no harm to the diet.)
serving of fresh strawberries or other fruit
coffee, tea or milk

Lunch

salad of chopped up vegetables in sour cream—(Vegetables can include
    cucumbers, green onions, radishes, tomatoes, and green peppers
    and celery stalks cut up.)
a slice of Cheddar cheese
2 pieces of rye crisp or Zwieback toast
skimmed milk, coffee, or tea

Dinner

Japanese beef and peppers on rice (recipe below)
diced cooked carrots
beef broth
vanilla ice milk or dietetic canned fruits for dessert
coffee, tea or skimmed milk

Recipe for Japanese beef and peppers on rice (only 200
calories per serving):

2 lbs. of ground round beef
1/2 teaspoon minced garlic
1 teaspoon salt substitute
2 beef bouillon cubes
1/2 teaspoon of powdered ginger
8 scallions, cut in pieces
4 celery stalks, cut in 1/2 inch pieces
4 medium green peppers, cut into strips
2 tablespoons of cornstarch
1 tablespoon of soy sauce
2 tablespoons of margarine

Shape the ground beef into small patties. Brown them in the
oil and minced garlic. Put in the beef cubes, ginger, salt and

pepper; cover with hot water and simmer for 15 minutes. Then add the vegetables and cook until vegetables are tender. Put the cornstarch, soy sauce and 1/2 cup of water together, and mix thoroughly, then add to the other ingredients in the skillet and cover it, cooking it about 10 more minutes, or until vegetables are tender.

SEVENTH DAY VARIATION DIET

Breakfast

> 1/2 honeydew melon
> 1/2 cup yogurt
> 1 slice whole-wheat or rye bread toasted
> coffee or tea

Lunch

> 1 cup of consommé
> two celery stalks and radishes
> calf's liver, broiled
> 4 wheat thins
> coffee or tea

Dinner

> 1 glass tomato juice
> baked bass, or other fish, broiled or baked only
> 1/2 cup of brown rice with margarine over it
> fresh fruit, or one-half canned peach
> coffee or tea

Between meals, while on this variation diet, you can eat a bowl of the reducing soup whenever you feel hungry. These variation diets can also be interspersed with the regular reducing diets given in the second chapter, to add variety and to help sustain you if you have to go beyond the 7-day period of dieting.

Later I shall give many other menus that will add variety to your regular meals when you go on the sustaining diet to maintain your normal weight.

OTHER POINTERS TO FOLLOW
DURING THE 7-DAY DIET

1. Avoid table salt, which is sodium chloride, and use a salt substitute, if you eat at home. If you eat in restaurants the food will already be salted, so avoid putting extra salt on the food.

Your body can absorb only 300 grains of salt a day, and each shake on the salt-cellar gives about 1000 grains. The excess salt is stored in the body tissues with large quantities of liquids. This is why the first two or three days of fasting and dieting generally make you lose three or four pounds of weight—most of it is water that has been held in solution in the tissues by the salt you have ingested for years.

2. Avoid reducing pills or other drugs while you are on this diet. (Exceptions: those who have diabetes or other illnesses that require a doctor's care.) Check with your doctor before you embark on any reducing diet, and occasionally while on the diet, to be sure you are maintaining your usual level of energy and good health.

3. Should you take vitamins while on this Oriental reducing diet? I always suggest that you take a good vitamin pill that contains all the essential vitamins, minerals, and other elements that have been judged as being essential to good health. However, avoid overdoing, as it has now been found by medical research that most people overdo in taking vitamins without a doctor's advice and more harm can be done than good. Later we shall discuss vitamins in further detail.

4. If you feel weak after a day or two of this reducing diet and you want a quick pick-up, do not mistakenly eat sugar or candy, or honey, thinking your body needs sugar for quick energy. Your body needs the sugar that comes from natural fruits or fruit juices. But rather than drink too much fruit juice while on this diet, eat the natural oranges or other fruits, whenever possible. The reason for this is simple: The juices are quickly absorbed into your system and require no digestion whereas the whole fruits, with their pulp, require a longer time to digest and make the stomach work. If you eat an apple when hungry, or stewed apples, or baked apples without sugar, your body is given quick energy without adding to the fat problem.

5. Avoid eating anything just before retiring at night. The body requires very few calories while you sleep and these are adequately furnished by your normal evening meal.

If you do feel hungry at night or during the night, drink a glass of skimmed milk or eat some kind of fruit, such as melon, apples, two or three prunes, dried apricots or fruits in season. You can also nibble on a piece of cheese to appease your appetite.

—6—

What You Should Know About Calories, Vitamins and Foods to Never Again Put on Weight

The biggest problem facing any dieter is the fact that he can, and often does take off weight following this Oriental 7-day system of dieting, but within a few weeks' time, through carelessness or not knowing food values, he puts the weight back on again.

It is disheartening to lose weight and then see the scales registering those lost pounds in a few weeks' time. This is why it is vitally important that you know the truth about calories, vitamins, minerals and foods in general, so that you can go on a sustaining diet that will be nutritious and at the same time keep the unwanted pounds off.

Although you do not need to count calories during the 7-day quick weight-off diet given in this book, it is important that you know something about calories so you can avoid overloading the body with unneeded calories in the future. It must always be remembered that even if you ate nothing but meat and overate large quantities, absorbing more calories than the body can use, the extra calories would be stored by the body as fat. Of course, carbohydrates, starches and sugars convert into fat much quicker than lean meat, and these should be lowered drastically on any sustaining diet to keep your body at normal weight.

The recommended calories per day for the average person, released recently by scientific sources are as follows: 2,200 to 2,900 calories for U.S. men, depending on their weight, age and height. The recommended number of calories per day for the average woman is between 1,600 and 2,100 calories.

Men who do heavy labor require up to 3,500 calories a day to keep them in good condition. If they consume 4,000 or more calories a day they are going to put on excess weight. In this category of heavy labor I would include people who use their muscles in lifting or moving heavy objects, like furniture, machinery or packing crates filled with heavy objects. Truck drivers who do not lift heavy loads, but merely drive their trucks, would hardly be classified as heavy laborers. They actually have sedentary jobs and require no more than 2,500 calories per day. This is one reason why most truck drivers you see on the road weigh from 25 to 80 pounds too much. They stop at roadside cafes to eat mostly carbohydrate foods such as sandwiches, pies, cakes, ice cream, coffee and doughnuts and other starches. They do not need all those fat calories and the body stores them as fat.

You can cut out at least 50 percent of the carbohydrates you would normally eat on the sustaining diet and this will help you keep the body at its normal weight. This, of course, means that you should balance the diet with adequate amounts of proteins, vegetables and fruits.

Each day part of this calorie content taken by men and women should be of a high protein nature. It is estimated that men require at least 350 protein calories a day and that women require at least 290 protein calories. No adequate research has ever been made on the carbohydrate requirements per day. If you play safe by keeping on a very low carbohydrate diet, you will get immediate results in your program for losing weight. This is why the Oriental 7-day diet works miracles—it furnishes the body with the vegetables and meat protein, allowing for a small intake of carbohydrates in the brown rice, with plenty of fats and sugars for energy, in the ingestion of some oils and fruits or natural desserts that give blood sugar for energy without danger of storing the excess sugar as fat.

The basic reason for people being overweight is the fact that their bodies do not burn up carbohydrates easily and store these calories as fat. This is one good reason for reducing the intake of carbohydrates and substituting the meat, vegetables and natural fruits for a maintenance diet that will be nutritious and yet keep off future weight.

One of the main worries of many people who undertake this 7-day Oriental diet is whether they will obtain sufficient vitamins and minerals while on the diet. They often ask: Are vitamins necessary as a daily supplement to the reducing diet and afterwards on the sustaining diet?

It has been scientifically established that the body requires certain vitamins and minerals, which could normally be supplied by food, if we all ate correctly. But this is difficult to do and it is recommended by most doctors and nutritionists that supplementary vitamins be taken while on reducing diets and then followed up on the sustaining diet. Here is the logical reason for this: During the many years of reaping crops without enriching the soil, we have witnessed a gradual deterioration of the soil, especially in this country. Although now the farmers are trying to restore the balance with fertilizers many people feel that artificial fertilizers do more harm than good. The foods are then further processed and devitalized in our modern manufacturing plants and many believe that they are robbed of their nutritive elements and most of the vitamins and minerals are destroyed.

Fruits, which normally would be nourishing if allowed to ripen on the trees, are picked while unripe and allowed to ripen in the markets. All these practices tend to destroy nature's balance and make many of our processed foods lack vitamins and minerals which they should have.

HOW THREE INTERNATIONAL STARS
RETAIN THEIR SLENDER FIGURES

Once when I was living in Athens, I was invited to a big party on board the *Christina,* the private yacht of billionaire Aristotle

Onassis. This was when he was still married to his first wife, Christine, and before Jacqueline Kennedy. As I knew most of the American colony stationed in Athens, it was a common occurence to be invited to all the embassy parties and to meet international figures in that center of civilization, the crossroads of the world.

I remember on this beautiful summer day there were three international celebrities on that yacht, two of whom I had met in my Hollywood years when I was the advisor to the movie stars. These were Greta Garbo and Elizabeth Taylor. Miss Taylor had been making the picture *Cleopatra* in Rome and flew over for the special party. The other guest was a completely new and slenderized Maria Callas, whom I had seen in concert when she weighed more than 200 pounds.

It was good talking over old Hollywood days with the two famous movie stars, but what was more interesting was to observe that all three of these international stars had retained their looks and figures! Maria Callas admitted she had a struggle, for until she got off the rich Greek foods, with their oils and carbohydrates, she simply could not lose weight.

I have never seen a fat Garbo, in all the years I've seen her in Hollywood and on the international scene. Garbo lives strictly according to the natural food plan, and has never had a weight problem. But Elizabeth Taylor confessed that she had to watch her weight constantly, for if she ate the things she liked, which were usually in the fat and carbohydrate class, she would gain weight overnight.

As for Aristotle Onassis, here I observed, was a dynamo of energy and power, and I carefully observed the diet that seemed to be followed on the yacht, and I knew that he also was well aware of the right foods to eat and to avoid.

The luncheon began with a vast variety of salads and fruits laid out on a long table, smorgasbord style. I noticed that our three international celebrities only nibbled at these appetizers, preferring the fresh salads and fruits to the heavier starchy appetizers.

Then at the table the salad was served and it was a big bowl filled with fresh cut up vegetables, and tender, tiny shrimp, right fresh from the Aegean Sea. Over this was a French dressing.

The main course consisted of barbecued young lamb, served with fresh asparagus tips, with a special white sauce that was delicious.

For dessert everyone felt that the choice was an especially good one, on such a big meal, for it consisted of large, ripe strawberries, in a big champagne glass with imported French champagne poured over them. It was a perfect meal and I noticed that even Garbo partook of everthing, but in small portions.

Later, I asked Elizabeth Taylor what her favorite dessert was, and she remarked, "It's not a slenderizing one, I'm afraid, but I love fresh pineapple with sour cream over it. When we cannot get fresh pineapple, we use the pineapple chunks canned, with the syrup washed off. Its simply delicious!"

PROOFS OF VALUE OF VITAMINS AND MINERALS

For many years scientists attempted to prove the need for vitamins and minerals in the human diet. They experimented at first with rats, and found that when they were deprived of certain elements in their daily diets they suffered from every known complaint from arthritis to sterility. But people said, "Rats are not human beings, and they do not react in the same way to dietary deficiencies."

It was then that scientists began to experiment with vitamin therapy on human beings and they soon found out that what applied to animals, such as rats, in their laboratory experiments, also applied to human beings.

When vitamins were restricted in human nutrition it was found that people became highly nervous and neurotic. They tired easily, had no resistance to disease, caught colds quickly, especially when deprived of the important Vitamin C in their diets. Calcium deficiencies soon produced difficulties in metabolism and nutrition, as well as tooth and bone formation.

Perhaps the greatest proof of the needs of certain vitamins and elements in the diet is that furnished by history. A naval doctor observed that the crews of British ships broke out in scurvy on long ocean voyages when they were denied fresh vegetables and fruits. He tried giving the sick men fresh lemons and the signs of scurvy completely disappeared.

Another scientist noted that when laboratory rats were given a diet of protein and carbohydrates, and nothing else, they became sick. He added whole milk to their diets and the rats became healthy once again. It was concluded then by scientists that in order to be healthy one required a diet made up of proteins and carbohydrates and certain other unknown elements. It was a Polish chemist named Casimir Funk who discovered what these other unknown elements were, so he named them vitamins.

Scientists estimate that there are 13 vitamins which are essential to good health. There have been as many as 50 vitamins isolated in recent years, but all of them are not considered essential to maintaining good health. Some scientists claim that at least 25 of these known vitamins are important to the proper functioning of the body.

We shall consider a few of these vitamins which have been proved essential to human nutrition. You may consult your doctor to see if you need special vitamin therapy, or if you can take one capsule a day, which contains most of the essential vitamins and minerals thought necessary for human nutrition. He will recommend the particular brand that he feels is best for your special needs.

Vitamin A

This is the vitally important vitamin that helps protect your body against infections. It is also thought that when the body does not have sufficient Vitamin A there may be deficiencies in fertilization and difficulties in the growth of the embryo in the mother's womb. This often causes childbirth disturbances.

Vitamin A is also thought to be important to full bone formation. A lack of this vitamin can also affect digestion adversely, and sometimes cause respiratory disturbances. It is also thought to affect premature aging and when sufficient quantities of Vitamin A are present in the diet, many scientists believe that it adds extra years to life.

How can you obtain Vitamin A from natural foods? You can find this important vitamin in many green vegetables, including turnip greens, broccoli, squash, dandelions, collards, and mustard greens.

Vitamin A is also found in carrots, apricots, cantaloupes, and other yellow fruits and vegetables. Fish liver oils, liver, eggs, cream and butter are also heavy in Vitamin A. It is estimated by scientists that the human body puts fat on more rapidly when it is deprived of Vitamin A, and they recommend at least 10,000 units a day.

Vitamin B₁ (Thiamine)

The B vitamins are all essential to good health and a balanced nutrition. However, Vitamin B_1, which contains thiamine, seems to be necessary for the proper functioning of the heart muscle and the body muscles as well as the entire nervous system. It also regulates the action of the adrenal glands when there is danger or threat to a person.

Modern research on this important vitamin shows that a lack of it causes a person to lose his sexual desires. The symptoms of a lack of Vitamin B_1 are irritability, quick temper, nervousness, fatigue, constipation, indigestion, distended abdomen, a loss of desire for food, and very often, dry hair.

Vitamin B_1 has been called the vitality vitamin by some, and it can be obtained in its natural form in such foods as soybeans, brown rice, wheat germ, brewer's yeast, beef kidneys, beef heart, oysters, some pork products and in eggs. As this vitamin is easily destroyed by heat, one should avoid overcooking and be sure to get it in such foods as yeast, wheat germ, and oysters eaten on the half shell.

Vitamin B₂ (Riboflavin)

When this vitamin is missing in the diet it can affect the eyes, often causing burning, itching and a bloodshot condition. It is also a good skin tonic. When there is a lack of this important vitamin the body seems to age faster and has less resistance to fatigue. Very often its lack shows in skin disorders, such as dandruff and eczema. Scientists noted that lack of this vitamin can also cause mental depression, loss of hair, and a general diminished vitality that affects sexual potency.

This vitamin can be obtained in the following foods: milk, eggs, cheese, wheat germ, brewer's yeast, liver, green vegetables, peas, lima beans, yogurt, whole-wheat cereals and flour. If you eat plenty of yeast and liver you will obtain adequate amounts of riboflavin in your diet.

Vitamin B_6 (Known as Pyridoxine)

Until recently this little known vitamin was not thought to be important to human nutrition. Recent research shows that pyridoxine is important to the metabolism of proteins and helps form antibodies that can fight germ infections, and aid in healing. It has also been found to have a sedative effect on the nerves, and improves muscle tone. It is being widely used today in the treatment of muscular dystrophy and multiple sclerosis, as well as in other disorders affecting the nerves and muscles.

This vitamin is to be found in whole-wheat foods, bran and cereals, as well as in most meats. Liver is very high in this vitamin, and so are fresh, green, leafy vegetables.

Niacin (Vitamin B)

Niacin is part of the entire B complex and is essential in the diet to oxidize carbohydrates and to build enzymes that give mental well-being, as well as a healthy skin. Niacin is vitally important to the operation of the human brain and the nervous system. When it is lacking in the human diet it often leads to nervous disorders that can range from simple nervousness to insanity. It can also contribute to hair growth and healthy hair through its effect on the blood's circulation to the scalp.

Niacin can be found in natural foods such as liver, lean meats, fish, poultry, bran and yeast. It also exists in the leafy green vegetables.

Vitamin B_{12}

Since 1948, when this vitamin was first isolated, it was recommended for the treatment of pernicious anemia. Now it has been found that this vitamin is essential for the proper functioning of the body's metabolism. When there are sufficient quantities of this vitamin in the human diet it gives mental alertness and physical vigor. It has also been found essential in normal functioning of bone marrow as it contains an essential element, cobalt. This vital vitamin has been found to stimulate growth in retarded children. When this essential vitamin is lacking in the diet it has been found to create disturbances in the nervous system and deprives one of the true enjoyment that comes from sexual relations. It has also been found necessary to avoid pernicious anemia.

This vitally important vitamin is not to be found in vegetables. It is found only in meat, especially liver, and milk. The organ meats are especially good sources. Also it can be found in fish, eggs, and milk products such as cottage cheese and yogurt.

OTHER B VITAMINS

Most vitamin tablets on the market today contain other members of the B vitamin family, which some consider essential to human nutrition. Following is a brief description of these vitamins in the B complex, and what is known about their effects on human nutrition.

Pantothenic Acid

This form of the B complex vitamin affects the absorption of carbohydrates and the body's metabolism. It also has a strong effect on the functioning of the adrenal glands, which secrete the hormone substance known as adrenalin. Pantothenic acid is also thought to be important for mental health, as it reacts favorably on the nervous system and when the mind and body are under stress conditions. Some research has been done in the field of gray hair and pantothenic acid and it is claimed that lack of this B vitamin in the diet often leads to premature graying of the hair.

Pantothenic acid is found in liver, kidney, heart, yeast, egg yolk, black molasses, rice bran and wheat bran, peas and peanuts.

Choline

This member of the B complex family is said to be important in the absorption of fats and also prevents fatty degeneration of the liver. It is also said to control the transmission of nerve impulses from the brain to the body's muscles and organs. Choline is to be found in its natural state in beef heart, egg yolk, legumes, whole-grain cereals, and green vegetables.

Inositol

This B complex vitamin seems to join in with choline to help the body absorb fatty foods, and also to protect the liver. It has been found important also to help the stomach pass food through the intestines through a process known as peristalsis. It is to be found in organ meats, most meats, soy beans, citrus fruits and cereal brans.

Folic Acid

This is the B complex vitamin that is thought by scientists to be important to the building of normal red blood cells, and it also helps fight anemia. It gives the body the ability to fight stress conditions produced by modern living, and helps build antibodies that fight germ invasion of the body. It can be found in such foods as liver, organ meats, kidneys, yeast and to some extent in green leafy vegetables, whole wheat, veal, beef and salmon.

Biotin

This B complex vitamin is important to the proper functioning of the enzymes in the body fluids and also assists the respiratory system. It can be obtained in most meats, in liver and kidneys, in egg yolk, yeast, vegetables, milk, nuts, grains and molasses.

You can use wheat and corn germ as a daily food supplement to assure that you are getting many of the important vitamin B family in your diet. Use wheat germ or corn germ over your salads and use wheat germ instead of bread crumbs to coat fish, veal or other meats when you want to bake or fry them.

Add a tablespoon of food yeast to your stews, gravies, and even tomato juice.

Eat at least two glasses of yogurt a day while on your sustaining diet, and also use yogurt instead of mayonnaise or sour cream to make your salad dressings.

Try to eat broiled liver at least twice a week, and remember, beef liver is just as good as calf's liver, and less expensive.

Vitamin C

There has been a great deal of controversy regarding Vitamin C in relation to building the body's immunity to colds and infections. However, scientists think it has other important functions in the human body and is essential in the diet.

Vitamin C has to do with building resistance to infections, and also the body's healing. It helps maintain the cartilage, bones and teeth in good condition. It also helps support the body's network of small blood vessels, veins and capillaries in good condition, and causes them to function more efficiently.

Vitamin C is not stored in the body and has to be supplied daily through the diet or through other sources.

Vitamin C is to be found abundantly in all citrus fruits, oranges, lemons, grapefruit, tomatoes, limes, raspberries, black currants, raw cabbage, green peppers, cauliflower, kale, parsley, watercress, broccoli, spinach and new potatoes.

Vitamin D

This is thought to be essential for the formation of good bones and teeth, and also for calm nerves and to assist the body to achieve normal growth. It also helps the metabolism in the absorption of phosphorus and calcium.

Vitamin D is called the "sunshine vitamin," because it is contained in abundance in the sun's rays and those who sunbathe a good deal absorb this important vitamin. It can also be obtained in capsules of fish liver oils. Only a few foods contain this important vitamin: irradiated yeast, eggs, milk, and in such fish as tuna, salmon, sardines and mackerel.

Vitamin E

This vitamin is considered essential to the normal functioning of the cardiovascular system. It is often called the sex vitamin and it is thought to be important in maintaining sexual potency as well as for the proper functioning of the reproductive glands. When there is a lack of Vitamin E in animals it has been found that it leads to a degeneration of the testicles and sterility. Now many doctors are treating impotency in men and frigidity in women with diets rich in Vitamin E. It is also thought important for the control of unpleasant symptoms in menopause by eliminating hot flashes, excessive menstrual flow and backache. When taken with Vitamin A, it is also found to help protect one against liver disorders, dry skin, persistent headaches, and it is said to be an aid in hair and skin beauty.

Vitamin E is to be found in wheat germ and oil, corn germ and oil, soya oil, muscular meats, nuts, eggs, legumes and green leafy vegetables.

Vitamin F

This vitamin is a key factor in the absorption of other vitamins and it is said to distribute calcium; it also is a contributing factor to the maintenance of good health and growth. When this vitamin is lacking it is found that a person can have a tendency to arteriosclerosis. It helps the body resist disease and assists the body in maintaining its proper cholesterol level. This vitamin is found in grain and vegetable oils, wheat germ, safflower, peanut, soybean and sunflower oils. If these oils were used in salads and cooking they would supply the body's normal needs of Vitamin F.

Vitamin K

Scientists have recently reported that Vitamin K is important to the normal clotting of the blood and to prevent hemorrhage. In Japan recently, scientists claimed that Vitamin K is vitally important in human longevity. This vitamin is to be found in spinach, kale, cabbage, tomatoes, soy beans, liver and vegetable oils. It is also to be found in egg yolk and alfalfa.

Vitamin P

This vitamin is essential to the normal health of the capillary system and is thought to be important to sexual arousal. It has another vital function—cell feeding and the removal of waste products from the body. It also gives protection against many diseases and the malfunctioning of many of the body's vital processes. It is to be found in plums, prunes, grapes, spinach, parsley, green peppers, citrus fruits, lettuce, cabbage, watercress, cabbage, apples and carrots. Paprika is also a good source of this vitamin.

THE IMPORTANCE OF MINERALS IN ANY DIET

Most people know a great deal about the importance of vitamins in the diet, but little about minerals. These are now considered important in the diet for minerals and vitamins work together. There are at least 16 minerals in our foods, but we will consider only eight of the most important ones. Again, these are generally included in modern packaging of vitamins but they can also be obtained from natural foods.

Calcium

Calcium is well known as the builder of the bones and teeth and for the maintenance of the body's skeletal structure. Calcium, in conjunction with Vitamin D, is important to the body for it helps the body absorb calcium from the stomach and digestive tract and helps the body utilize it. It has also been found that calcium is vitally essential to a balanced, calm nervous system.

Calcium needs to be replenished often, for if the body lacks this vital mineral, it borrows it from your bones to make up for its lack in foods.

Calcium is found plentifully in the following foods: milk, most cheeses, blackstrap molasses, buttermilk, lemons, oranges, powdered skim milk, yogurt, leafy vegetables, cottage cheese, seafood, whole grains, egg yolk and poultry.

Iron

Iron is essential in the diet because it helps the blood carry oxygen throughout the body and also helps eliminate carbon dioxide from the body's cells.

Iron is essential to avoid anemia and to maintain the bloodstream in good health. It also contributes to quicker thinking and gives the body more vital energy.

Foods that are rich in iron are: liver, yeast, blackstrap molasses, barley, wheat germ, whole wheat, dried apricots and peaches, navy and kidney beans, soy beans, lean meats, bran, eggs, lentils, oysters, prunes and raisins.

Iodine

Iodine is thought vitally important for the normal functioning of the thyroid gland and to help the body's metabolism. When people are easily fatigued and feel a let-down around mid-day, it is usually because they lack this vital mineral in their diets. When a severe case of iodine deficiency exists it can even lead to the formation of goiter. Iodine can be found in seafoods, principally shrimps, lobster, oysters, sea greens and iodized salt.

Phosphorus

It is thought that phosphorus works like calcium in the body, and is closely associated with it in sustaining the fluid content of the brain. It also helps reinforce the nerves and muscles. It aids the glands in their proper secretions and assists the muscles in their contractions. It is to be found in the following foods: meats, fish, eggs, cheese, poultry, and whole wheat and soybeans.

Manganese

The first place that an absence of this vital mineral is noticed is in a loss of interest in sex. When it is lacking in the diet it can impair normal reproductive functions and often lessens the maternal instinct in women. This vital mineral activates the enzymes and works with calcium and phosphorus. It is to be found in whole grains, cereals, and green vegetables.

Copper

This mineral helps avoid anemia for it works in conjunction with iron. This mineral also plays a part in pigment formation and a deficiency in copper can sometimes lead to premature gray hair. Copper is to be found in the same foods that are rich in iron, and also in oatmeal and huckleberries.

Sodium

Sodium is essential to the absorption of all the other minerals by the body. Sodium is plentiful in celery, green string beans and kelp or sea salt.

Potassium

This mineral is called nerve food, for it helps the nerves, assists the heart and muscles, and is generally important in avoiding indigestion, constipation, and insomnia, nervousness and irritability. Potassium is found in green leafy vegetables, carrots, cucumbers, kelp, cranberries, tomatoes, apple cider vinegar, blackstrap molasses, honey and many fruits.

With this knowledge to fortify you, you can make your own decision as to whether you need vitamin and mineral supplements in your reducing or maintenance diet. You may feel that you obtain sufficient amounts in your normal diet of both vitamins and minerals. If there is any doubt or you have some special condition that gives you problems, be sure to consult your family physician for more specific guidance on this matter.

— 7 —

Exciting New Dishes to Supplement the Oriental Quick Weight Loss Plan

One of the most difficult things for a dieter to face is the deadly monotony of any reducing diet. The Oriental food plan is no exception to this rule. However, using our basic diet for reducing without hunger, we can add exciting new dishes to this plan that give nourishing meals as well as exciting the taste buds so you can alternate the 7-day plan by using any of the following dishes.

These dishes, using the basic oriental diet plan, will give variety to your reducing menus, without fear of adding weight.

Fish is one of the best sources for high protein in any reducing diet. There is a wide variety of this delicious protein food available and it may be prepared in many tasty dishes that can add variety to your *reducing without hunger* diet.

A delicious reducing salad may be prepared for guests, who will never suspect you are on a diet, as follows:

Shanghai tuna and shrimp salad to be served on a bed of cold lettuce.
Two or three cans of white meat chunk tuna.
One pound of cooked shrimps.
One small chopped up onion.
Bits of green pepper or red pepper to add color, chopped up fine.
Add dried tarragon, or a touch of tarragon vinegar to the following
reducing mayonnaise.

REDUCING MAYONNAISE

2 tbs. of tarragon vinegar or lemon juice
1 egg yolk
1 tsp. honey
1/2 tsp. salt or substitute
1 tsp. dry mustard
1/2 tsp. ginger
touch of black pepper
1/4 tsp. paprika
1/4 tsp. basil
1 cup soy oil

Blend these ingredients in a blender, all except the oil, which
should be added slowly while blending the other ingredients. Add
the oil slowly, and also half the vinegar, until the mixture begins
to thicken and then add all the oil.

Mix the ingredients of the salad with enough homemade
mayonnaise to make it tasty and serve on a bed of cold lettuce.

LOBSTER CANTONESE

You can use frozen lobster tails for this delicious protein
substitute in your reducing diet or in the sustaining diet, as it is
nourishing without adding weight.

6 Rock Lobster tails (remove the undershell)
3/4 cup of salad oil
juice of one lemon
3/4 tsp. salt or salt substitute
2 large minced garlic cloves
1/8 tsp. of black pepper
several sprigs of chopped parsley

Mix the ingredients in a bowl and marinate the lobster tails in this mixture for about one hour. Then broil them in a hot oven, shell side up. Serve with lemon and butter sauce. (Or you may use margarine and lemon.)

INDONESE FILLETS OF FISH IN WINE SAUCE

1 lb. of fish fillets
1 onion, chopped fine
1 tbs. margarine
1 garlic clove, minced
1/2 cup of white wine
1 tbs. chopped parsley
1 medium can of tomatoes
1/4 spoonful oregano
2 tbs. cream
add salt and pepper to taste

Fillets are first cut in half. Brown the onion and garlic in a pan with margarine. Cover the fish with tomatoes, wine and parsley. Cover and simmer after bringing to a boil over low fire for about 20 minutes. Then add the oregano and cream, stirring it together until it is smooth. Garnish with parsley and serve.

SINGAPORE PORK BAKED OVER CHARCOAL

2 lbs. of lean pork (to serve about 6 guests)
1 cup of salted almonds
2 cloves of garlic, minced
2 tbs. ground coriander seeds
crushed red pepper
3 medium sized onions chopped fine
3 tbs. lemon juice
2 tbs. brown sugar
1/4 cup soy sauce
1/2 cup melted margarine
1/2 cup chicken bouillon
salt and pepper to taste
(To be served on a bed of cooked brown rice when finished.)

Cut the pork into cubes about 1 inch square. (Trim off all fat.) Put all the ingredients except the chicken bouillon and margarine into a blender and make a puree of it. Boil this and then add the melted margarine and bouillon. Let this mixture cool, and then pour over the chunks of pork and let stand two hours. Put the meat on iron skewers and broil over charcoal fire. Use the leftover sauce to baste occasionally while cooking and then serve on a bed of brown rice, with the balance of the sauce.

CURRY OF LOBSTER INDIENNE

This delicious dish may often be substituted for the other forms of meat to add variety in your 7-day diet. Or if you continue the reducing diet to a two or three week period it is important that you use these variations to your regular diet plan or you will suffer from the usual monotony that afflicts most dieters and makes them give up before achieving their desired weight loss.

3 or 4 lbs. of parboiled lobster	pinch of salt
2 sliced tomatoes	1 tsp. sugar
2 sliced onions	1 tbs. lemon juice
pinch of cinnamon	2 cloves garlic minced
cumin	4 cups of skimmed milk
chili powder	1 cucumber
6 tbs. margarine	1 tbs. turmeric
1 tbs. coriander	

Fry the sliced onions with the cloves, cumin, chili, coriander, and cinnamon, turmeric and tomatoes in the 3 tbs. of margarine. Then add the sugar, salt, lemon juice and milk to this mixture. Simmer on low heat for 15 minutes. Then add the other 3 tbs. of margarine in another pan and slightly fry the garlic in it. Then add the lobster and coat it well with margarine (or if you wish, you may use real butter for this). Cook for only five or six minutes, then add the milk and spices. Cook until the liquid has been reduced by almost 1/3. Keep pan covered while cooking. Then add thinly sliced cucumbers to the lobster and cook for an additional 10 minutes. It may be served on a bed of cooked brown rice.

ORIENTAL GREEN PEPPERS AND BEAN SPROUTS

To add variety to your lunches while reducing, you can serve this delicious dish for guests who need never know you are on a reducing diet. This may be served as the vegetable dish with a tuna salad or some other form of broiled fish.

    2 cups of canned bean sprouts (being sure to rinse them and remove the
        juice)
    2 tsp. sherry extract
    2 tsp. soy sauce
    1 medium green pepper cut in rings
    season with salt
    1 tsp. vinegar

Cook together the soy sauce, bean sprouts, green peppers, and sherry extract over moderate heat for about 15 minutes. Then add vinegar and salt and serve as a side dish to either a fish or lean meat meal.

JAPANESE FISH FILLETS AND GREEN PEAS

This delicious fish dish can be served for either lunch or dinner. In addition, to add filler, you may take a bowl of brown rice or another vegetable from our reducing list of vegetables, such as asparagus, spinach, cabbage or celery.

    2 lbs. of fish fillets cut up in 2 x 3 inch pieces
    1 cup of chicken bouillon
    1 clove minced garlic
    5 oz. sliced scallions
    2 tbs. minced ginger root or 1/4 tsp. ground ginger
    1 tsp. salt
    1 tsp. soy sauce
    1 tsp. artificial sweetener, or enough to equal 1 tsp. sugar

In a teflon pan cook together the chicken bouillon and the ginger root until it comes to a boil. Then add scallions, garlic and fish chunks, cooking lightly for about 5 minutes. When the fish flakes easily, add peas, soy sauce, sugar, and salt. Cook only about 5 minutes. Then serve. Makes about 4 servings.

VEAL ORIENTALE

Veal is an excellent form of meat while on this Oriental reducing diet. It can be combined with the vegetables in our reducing list and can also be served with a bowl of rice. This dish is easy to prepare and adds variety for the taste buds.

2 pieces of boneless veal (cut into 1 inch cubes)
4 tsp. sherry extract
1/2 cup water
1/4 cup soy sauce
2 tbs. salt or substitute
2 slices of ginger root or a pinch of ground ginger
1 tsp. artificial sweetener
garnish with watercress

In a saucepan brown the veal thoroughly over low fire. Add the water and sherry, soy sauce, salt and ginger. Mix thoroughly, and then add the browned veal. Reduce heat after bringing to a boil, and cook over low heat for 1 hour, covered. Then add the sweetener, and cook until tender, which should be about 1/2 hour longer. Serve on a bed of brown rice, with watercress garnishing.

HONG KONG PORK AND VEGETABLES

3 medium green peppers, cut in strips
2 lbs. lean pork, sliced thin
1 cup of sliced mushrooms
1/8 tsp. black pepper
1/8 tsp. ground ginger
1/8 tsp. nutmeg
1 tbs. soy sauce
1 cup onion bouillon or onion soup
2 pimentos cut into pieces (for garnishing)
2 cups of brown rice (to be served as side dish)

Combine the onions, green peppers, mushrooms, celery, salt, pepper, ginger, onion bouillon, nutmeg, sherry extract and soy sauce. Cover over and cook on low fire for 10 minutes. By this time the onions and celery should be tender but not overcooked.

Now add the pork and pimentos, and mix well, cooking for an additional four or five minutes.

Serve with brown rice as side dish.

Another excellent Oriental diet dish consists of Celestial shrimp and bamboo shoots. You may obtain these in most markets in cans. This can be served as the main dinner dish with a generous helping of brown rice with soy sauce. You will need:

2 lbs. of cooked shrimp
1 tablespoon soy sauce
4 tsp. sherry extract
8 oz. scallions cut up
1 tsp. artificial sugar
1/2 tsp. black pepper

Combine the soy sauce, sherry extract and artificial sweetener in a pan, with black pepper. In another pan put the shrimp, bamboo shoots and scallions. Then pour the sauce over the shrimp and cook over low heat for about 5 or 6 minutes. Serve with dish of brown rice on the side.

INDONESE BARBECUED CHICKEN

2 lbs. of boned chicken (serves 4—if you wish to serve 8, double recipe)
1/2 tsp. cumin
1/2 tsp. minced garlic
6 oz. water
3/4 tsp. vinegar
salt to taste

Cut the chicken into pieces of about 2 inches square and place them on skewers. Dip the chicken in the sauce made of the above ingredients, and cook for about 20 minutes over an open fire. Make the following sauce to serve with chicken.

1/2 cup chicken bouillon
5 tbs. peanut butter
1 tsp. sugar substitute
1 clove minced garlic
1 tsp. soy sauce
dash of paprika
4 oz. milk
1 bay leaf

Mix these sauce ingredients thoroughly and cook slightly, until they are blended. Then serve this sauce hot over the chicken.

OYSTERS A LA ORIENTALE

Oysters may be used as a variation to the Oriental reducing diet, instead of meat. These are an excellent source of protein and other elements and are not fattening. For this dish you will need:

2 doz. oysters
1 cup sliced mushrooms
8 oz. milk
8 oz. buttermilk
3 tbs. margarine or butter
1/2 tbs. chopped parsley
2 red chili peppers, crushed
1 tsp. cumin seed
yolks of 2 eggs
4 oz. of cream substitute
salt to taste

Slightly cook the oysters in their own juice and a little water. Then drain them and mince the oysters. Put chopped parsley into the melted butter and fry for about 1/2 minute, then add the mushrooms.

Now combine the milk and buttermilk, adding about 2/3 cup at a time, being sure you boil away most of the liquid after each addition. Then add the cumin and 2 tbs. water. In the water you should have soaked the crushed peppers, and now you throw away the peppers and use the water. Beat the egg yolk with the cream, add to the mushroom mixture with oysters, and salt. Cover and cook for a few moments only, then serve with a side dish of brown rice.

A TYPICAL DAY'S VARIATION
DIET MENUS TO ADD VARIETY

When you have lost the desired number of pounds, it is time for you to think a little about your typical day's variation menus, to give joy to your life and to avoid adding those extra pounds again.

From the lists of foods given in these variation menus, here is a typical sample day. You can make up your own combinations, giving wide variations to the choices of meats, vegetables, and fruits, which will make up your main staple diet from now on.

Breakfast

You can begin your day with a wide variety of fruit juices, from orange, or grapefruit, to cranberry, or prune juice. If you can, however, eat the whole fruit, such as orange or grapefruit, for the stomach has to work harder to digest it, whereas the juices are assimilated immediately.

If you want to drink delicious coffee without cream, you can do what the French do—use half skimmed milk and half coffee. Be sure the milk is hot, and instead of white sugar, use either artificial sugar or a small spoonful of honey. If you are a heavy worker and feel the need for more energy, you might take a poached egg, with two pieces of lean bacon, being sure all the fat is cooked out. (But also remember, you need about 2 tablespoonsfuls of fat a day to maintain your body at normal.) You can use a little butter on two pieces of whole-wheat toast.

Luncheon

At lunch you can use one of the delicious salad bowls that can be made with cut up breast of chicken, or tuna or shrimp, with chunks of cucumber and ripe tomatoes sprinkled through it. Choose one of the low-calorie dressings to put over it. This, with a piece of date bread, or whole-wheat bread, and a simple fruit cup for dessert, will hold the weight down and also hold you until dinner time.

As a mid-meal snack, to keep your energy high, you can choose a favorite flavored fruit yogurt or hot tea; you might even try a mint or jasmine tea, flavored with a spoonful of honey, a glass of tomato juice, or some other vegetable juice. You could eat a cupful of cottage cheese, or nibble on a cube of Cheddar cheese to kill your appetite, without adding too many fat-producing calories.

Dinner

A green salad is essential for almost every dinner, to act as a buffer between your appetite and a desire for rich, fattening foods. You could start with a vegetable juice cocktail, and a low-calorie dressing over an asparagus and grapefruit salad.

For your main course you could have calf's or beef liver steaks, broiled, with broiled mushrooms, or bacon, with the fat cooked out. A baked potato with a spoonful of yogurt and a small patty of butter will make the potato delicious. Remember, if it comes to a choice for your carbohydrates for an evening meal, a potato is preferable to eating two slices of wheat bread, or hot buns. White flour is generally devitalized, while the potato retains its natural minerals and nutritious elements.

A fruit compote for dessert will top off this meal perfectly.

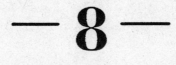

—8—

Additional
Quick Weight Loss Diets
Based on the
Oriental 7-Day Plan

If you really want to remain slender for the rest of your life and never again worry about putting on weight, this is possible with the Oriental quick weight loss rice diet. However, it does entail a strong will and you have to use many dietary tricks to keep your taste buds happy while going into these various diets.

A predominantly rice diet, either white or brown rice, with plenty of vegetables, is the basis of the Oriental system for losing weight. There are variations to the rice diet however, which you may want to apply from time to time.

Many years ago, when I first became interested in the Oriental system of losing weight and remaining slender, I remember reading an article in a national magazine written by a famous author. He told of how he suffered for years from being over-weight, with the usual symptoms of high blood pressure and other side effects. He came across the Oriental rice diet, with the addition of vegetables, vitamins and minerals, and went on this diet, with no meat, and drinking skimmed milk, and he told of how he lost many pounds of weight; his blood pressure returned to normal and he was able to do more work than ever before. Despite years of previous dietary abuses, he lived to be nearly 90 years of age and never again put on the undesired pounds during the rest of his life.

Men like George Bernard Shaw, and Mahatma Gandhi of India, were on a similar diet most of their lives and were slender, vital and youthful in appearance and had tremendous energy throughout their lives.

Heart trouble and high blood pressure are the modern killers in America today. Many doctors have subscribed to the rice diet to help those afflicted with these diseases.

Although rice diets were used by physicians primarily to treat high blood pressure cases, it was soon found that these predominantly rice diets had a wonderful side effect. Even though the patients consumed as much as 2,400 calories a day, they did not gain weight, but maintained the same weight.

Before embarking on these stringent diet plans to lose weight, you should always check with your personal doctor to see if you can take such a diet and have no special conditions that make it harmful. Then, when on the sustaining, predominantly rice diet, be sure you take one or two vitamin tablets a day, and as most vitamin tablets today contain the required amounts of minerals and other elements, you need not fear that you will become undernourished or sick from following these variations to the diet.

THE FIRST ALL RICE VARIATION DIET

This Oriental diet is the most stringent of all and should be used by any person who has 20 or more pounds to remove. If you want to lose the weight quickly, you can start this all rice diet and expect to shed the unwanted pounds more quickly than if you use the rice, fruits, vegetables and some meat diets given in the beginning of this book.

Prepare your brown rice in advance, and if you cannot buy brown rice in your grocery store, use the white rice. Cook it thoroughly, using no salt. (If you cannot stand the thought of saltless food, use the artificial salt which can be found in most markets.) As real salt often holds pounds of water in the body cells, it is a good idea to rid yourself of the salt habit in general, even when you are on the sustaining diet later, where you are permitted to add a variety of other foods to this basic rice diet.

During the day you can eat this rice diet whenever you feel hungry, three to six times a day. There is a built-in safety feature in this diet—*you can never eat too much rice!* Your appetite will not crave excessive amounts, but while on this quick weight loss diet, you will always feel full and never hungry. This is its great value.

You may drink 10 ounces of fruit juice during the day, at any time that you feel thirsty. This can be in the morning meal, or between meals. This can be any kind of fruit juice.

You may have 5 ounces of any fruits you choose, preferably fresh and in season. (To be eaten at or between meals.)

You can eat as much as 1/3 lb. of rice during the day, whenever you feel you are hungry. The rice can be given a variety of tastes by adding pineapple juice to it, a bit of margarine, or a small spoonful of honey.

You can drink all the water you want, all the coffee or tea, with artificial sugar and cream; you can also add two glasses of skimmed milk, to be taken between meals if you should be hungry.

This stringent rice diet should be taken without any vegetables whatsoever. It cannot harm you, if it is only indulged in for a period of three or four weeks. Remember, two-thirds of the people on earth subsist on a predominantly rice diet, and they are slender, have fewer diseases than Americans, and have energy enough to nearly conquer the world in war!

The wonderful thing about this drastic rice diet is that it will melt away at least 12 pounds the first week and possibly as many as 15 to 20 pounds in the next two weeks. Then you can stop this drastic plan and go on the sustaining diet, which will help you maintain your normal weight.

And remember, if you worry about protein lack in this diet, if you eat the brown rice instead of the processed white rice, you will be obtaining proteins and other nourishing elements in the brown rice that will give you many extra benefits.

THE SECOND VARIATION RICE DIET

In this plan you combine the brown or white rice and reducing vegetables, with fruit, fruit juices, and little else.

This diet plan is for those who only wish to lose 10 pounds or less, and who may not want to keep up the diet for more than a period of two weeks. It can also be used by those who want to lose from 20 to 50 pounds and who are willing to continue the 7-day plan for several additional weeks.

You can eat any of the following reducing vegetables on this reducing diet, and eat large portions, without fear of putting on pounds. The reason for this, as stated before, is that *the following vegetables require more calories to digest than they give to the body. You cannot overeat them.*

This diet assures you of always feeling comfortably full, and you need not worry about calories, for you will not be adding to your weight on these reducing, low-calorie vegetables.

The Power-Pack Reducing Vegetables

Following are the vegetables which you can eat in any quantities while on these predominantly rice diets without gaining one single ounce of weight. Use these vegetables with the second variation diet, and also with the third diet.

string beans	leeks	sauerkraut
broccoli	kohlrabi	tomatoes
cucumbers	green peppers	turnips
celery	lettuce	watercress
cabbage	mushrooms	radishes
asparagus	spinach	okra
garlic	dill pickles	brussel sprouts
lettuce		

The Power-Pack Reducing Fruits

You may use these fruits on all three diet plans, as they are reducing fruits and will not upset the reducing plan.

cantaloupe
pumpkin
honeydew melon
watermelon
rhubarb (sweetened with artificial sugar only)

On this variation diet number two, you may take the following at every meal:

8 ounces of fruit juice
4 ounces of fruits (but if you take the reducing fruits you can increase this, as these fruits on this list do not add weight, requiring more calories to digest than they give to the body)
All the steamed vegetables you desire in the above list (you may season the vegetables with artificial salt and a little margarine)
1/3 lb. of brown rice, with pineapple juice for flavor, or use margarine

Do NOT try to eat all the rice at one meal, for you will find it difficult if not impossible. Spread this 1/3 lb. of rice over four, or even five meals. You can skip it for breakfast, if you choose, and eat fruits and drink juices with your coffee or tea. Then in mid-morning you can take a portion of vegetables in the reducing list, with a bowl of warmed up rice. It will keep you from getting hungry all morning.

You may also drink beverages that are low in sugar, such as the dietetic drinks. Eat no fried foods on these variation rice diets, and avoid all desserts, outside of the permitted fruits. Be sure to take a therapeutic vitamin while on these rice variation diets.

THIRD VARIATION RICE DIET, FOR SLOWER REDUCING RESULTS

This next variation rice diet will also cause you to lose weight steadily and it gives a little more variety for your taste buds but it does add more calories for it includes fish and all varieties of lean meats, except pork. The meats must be broiled and all fat cut off.

Each day you can add (to the second variation rice diet) a four ounce portion of ground round steak, broiled; a piece of veal or beef; a small steak, broiled; or any of the following fish, which are very low in calories:

    sea bass
    cod steaks
    flounder
    raw oysters
    salmon (boiled)
    fresh tuna
    abalone
    shrimps, boiled or canned
    shad roe

The following meats may be added to this third variation diet, as they are low-calorie foods. Excessive amounts however, can quickly put the unwanted pounds back on, so use only small portions of about 4 ounces of these meats with the third variation rice diet.

    ground chuck (all fat removed)
    filet mignon
    heart
    kidney
    liver
    ground round
    pot roast
    sirloin steak, broiled
    sweetbreads
    T-bone steak
    tenderloin steak
    tripe
    lamb (lean)
    lamb chops, lean
    leg of veal or veal cutlets (roasted, with fat removed)

On this third variation diet, you can also add the following low-calorie dairy foods. You will still lose weight, but not as rapidly as on the first and second variation rice diets.

    cottage cheese
    skimmed milk
    buttermilk
    yogurt

You may also use eggs in this third variation rice diet—you

may eat a poached egg on rice for breakfast, or you may have an egg a day, if you decide you do not want to eat the meat and fish on this diet.

You may also add variety to this third rice diet by using any of the following fowl, being sure the skin, where most of the fat is to be found, is removed.

> broiled chicken, without stuffing
> roast turkey
> Cornish hens
> pheasant

While on any of these three variation rice diets avoid all of the following high-calorie fattening foods. This applies only to the period of dieting. When you have achieved your desired weight loss, you may add portions of these high-calorie fattening foods. They should always be used with great caution, however, for they are high in calories.

cube steak	fried lamb chops
hamburgers	roast lamb
porterhouse steak	sausages
rib roast	liverwurst, knockwurst
swiss steak	bologna
tongue	salami
boiled or fresh ham	processed meats of all kinds

THE FOURTH VARIATION RICE DIET FOR REDUCING

This diet is recommended for those who want to lose very little weight, and might even be taken as a sustaining diet, when you have lost your desired weight. It is a diet that adds much more variety to your meals and may be taken indefinitely to keep your weight at normal.

Keep on eating the brown rice, a little at each meal. This fills you up and makes you want less of the fattening foods, especially the carbohydrates and sugars and starches.

At each meal eat as much as you want of the fruits and vegetables given in the list of power-pack reducing vegetables. Eat any of the fruits given in the reducing list. Add to your daily diet lean meats, chicken, turkey, fish, cottage cheese, yogurt and skimmed milk. Avoid smoked fish or smoked meats while on this diet. Also avoid pork, ham, sausage, herring, salt, ketchup, pickles, and relishes and chili sauce.

While on any of these variation rice diets to lose weight, be sure to avoid all of the following foods. When you have lost the desired pounds you may use them at your discretion, always remembering they are the foods that put the weight on you in the first place and most of them should be eaten sparingly.

candies	gravies
cookies	mayonnaise
cakes	fatty meats
ice creams	meat pies
corn starch	all oils
crackers	popcorn
high calorie dressings on salads	sundaes
fried eggs	sugar
fried meats of all kinds	syrup
hominy	pretzels
banana fritters	white breads
pancakes or waffles	fatty soups

The following alcoholic beverages should be avoided while on this reducing plan:

beer	cognac	vermouth
ale	gin	vodka
brandy	rum	whiskey
champagne	sherry	dry wine
sweet wine		

— 9 —

The Vitalic Sustaining Diet to Keep Weight Off for the Rest of Your Life

The big fear that most people have after they have gone through the prolonged agony of losing weight is that it will come right back on again in a matter of a few weeks.

This is apt to be true if you return to your old habits of eating. The important thing to remember is that dieting can be maintained throughout your life without your suffering any harmful effects. You simply cut out the fat-calorie foods in your sustaining diet and replace them with the low-calorie foods. In this chapter we shall examine the vitalic sustaining diet that will keep you perfectly nourished without adding extra pounds for the rest of your life.

In any sustaining diet you use try to keep all fat intake at a minimum. It is true that you need some fat each day but it should be limited to about 60 grams a day. Most diets contain from 250 to 450 grams of fat each day. Any wonder that the body absorbs this unneeded fat and it is converted into unwanted pounds?

It is the high fat intake in the average American diet that leads to the deadly effects of cholesterol in the blood.

Hal T., a man whom I once knew, loved to eat fat meats. He would start his day with bacon and eggs; at lunch he ate meat again, with the fat left on it. His wife told me he would even take the fat off her plate at dinner, if she did not eat it.

Besides this heavy fat intake, this man was a heavy egg eater, usually having two or three at breakfast. He often varied this with several pancakes with heavy butter and syrup, and as many as three or four pork sausages.

This man was 45 years of age when he had his first heart attack. When I heard of it, I knew the reason for it. His cholesterol level had undoubtedly been so increased by his fat consumption that it affected his heart and blood pressure.

Hal weighed 220 pounds when he had his heart attack and the doctor told him he would have to go on a rigid diet to save his life. Fortunately, he took this advice seriously and it was at that time that his wife sought me out to find out if he should go on the Yoga diet, which I was then giving to thousands of my lecture members and class students at Carnegie Hall.

Hal began this Oriental system of dieting by reducing all fat intake immediately. He used the vegetable reducing soup, the brown rice, some vegetable fat in his salad dressings, and a 4 oz. piece of meat twice a day. The brown rice gave him such a feeling of satisfaction that he soon grew accustomed to going without excess fat. He had been eating as much as 500 grams of fat a day, and now, on the Oriental diet he was taking less than 60 grams a day. The first week of fasting and dieting, Hal lost 15 pounds, and then in the succeeding weeks he lost from 15 to 20 pounds, until he was down to 180 pounds, which was normal for his age and height. Hal's blood pressure dropped to normal and he had no recurrence of heart attacks in the next two years I observed him.

THE VITALIC FOODS THAT DO NOT PUT ON WEIGHT

Following are the foods you can eat the rest of your life that will keep you from putting on those extra pounds in the future. Most of these foods are in the regular Oriental quick-loss diet but now we shall add foods that give more low-fat calories as well as good nutrition.

The Value of Soups as Fillers

You can still take one or two bowls of soup a day while on the sustaining diet. However, now that the unwanted pounds are gone, you can switch from the power-pack reducing vegetables that add no calories, and take regular soups made with vegetables and lean meats. Be sure to skim off all fats that gather on such soups.

You can use vegetable broths, and creamed soups, but let the cream be skimmed milk.

Add to the sustaining diet the nourishing legume family to prepare your soups. Lentils are an excellent source of nourishment without adding fats. Cook the lentils with one large onion chopped up, artificial salt, and a small amount of polyunsaturated corn oil. (Remember, the body requires at least two tablespoons of fat or oil a day, so do not eliminate fat entirely in your cooking while on this sustaining diet.)

Make soups also from dried peas and navy beans. In the pea soup, as well as the lentil soup, you can add cut up pieces of lean frankfurters. Be sure they are beef, not pork. This soup can be eaten for a luncheon, with a small green salad, tea or coffee, and a gelatin dessert, made with artificial sugar. You will feel full and yet your body is not going to absorb many calories from this luncheon.

LARGE VARIETY OF MEATS POSSIBLE
WITH SUSTAINING DIET

Unfortunately, all meats, even when they seem to be lean, have veins of fat in them. As the meats are desirable forms of protein for any sustaining diet, it is important you choose those that are lean and prepare them in such a way that the fat will be cooked out.

If you use ground round or chuck, ask the butcher to trim all excess fats away.

Avoid frying all meats from now on, for this is one of the ways by which you absorb many fat calories that quickly bring back the unwanted pounds. You can cook meat without using fat in the pan. Sprinkle a little salt in the heated pan, put the meat in and turn it several times until cooked well.

There are now on the market one or two products which are recommended for low-fat cooking of meats or eggs. These are sprayed onto the frying pan and then the meat or eggs are cooked in it. The food will not stick to the pan.

Avoid the high fat and cholesterol meats such as pork chops, roast loin of pork, bacon and ham. The same thing applies to sausages, salami, liverwurst, brains, kidneys and sweetbreads. You can eat small quantities of these foods once a week to add variety to the diet but generally they should be avoided if you want to keep away from the high fat-calorie foods.

Liver is usually excellent, and can be broiled or fried in the above manner, without the use of fat.

To add to the appeal of your meat dishes while on the permanent sustaining diet, you can garnish your dishes with various types of fruits. If you use canned fruits be sure to wash out the excess sugars that are contained in the syrup. These add hundreds of unwanted calories and should be avoided. You can use sliced pineapple, purple plums, peach halves, prunes, or broiled bananas.

A good way to add variety to meat dishes also is through the use of various sauces, such as chili sauce, ketchup, relishes, jellies, applesauce, mint jelly, cranberry sauce and chutney.

Also to keep meats from tasting uniformily the same try adding herbs and spices to your cooking, such as garlic, basil, oregano, thyme and bay leaves. The Greek and Italian dishes frequently use these spices, especially oregano, to enliven their cooked meats, and they add nothing in the way of calories to the meat dishes.

USE POULTRY OF ALL KINDS
TO ADD TASTY PROTEINS

Your sustaining diet will vary greatly if you do not restrict yourself to the well-known meats. Use chicken, turkey, and squab or Guinea hen occasionally to give variety to your meat intake. If most of the fat is cooked out of the turkey or chicken in baking, rather than frying, it will add fewer calories. Duck is filled with too much fat, as is also goose, but for variety, small portions of these can be eaten once in a while without upsetting the diet.

You can use chicken and turkey for sandwiches and salads also, with a low-calorie mayonnaise. Be sure that you use the protein breads or the whole-wheat breads, and avoid white breads that have had all the nourishment processed out of them. An excellent lunch on this sustaining diet can be a chicken or turkey sandwich, with a small salad, a glass of whole milk, or coffee or tea; or, a chicken or turkey salad, with a low-calorie mayonnaise.

FISH DISHES BEST SOURCES OF PROTEINS
ON THE SUSTAINING DIET

Many nutritionists now claim that many types of fish are better protein sources, with less fat, than some of the meat proteins. However, if fish is fried, the fat calories are unnecessarily added. It is best to broil fresh fish, without the use of oil.

Flounder, perch, scallops, haddock and sturgeon are all excellent forms of protein with very little fat. You can eat small portions of fish like brook trout, porgy, cod and croakers, but they are a little higher in fat-calories than the above fish.

Lobster, crabs and shrimps are exceedingly low in fat-calories and cholesterol content. Clams are also excellent if eaten raw or in a stew. Fried, they become saturated in fat-calories. Oysters are also excellent eaten raw or in stews.

Tuna fish, fresh or canned, is generally low in fat-calories, although some brands of tuna, when packed in oil, do not fit in this category. Choose the brands that are not packed in oil. Sardines are high in fat-calories and should be eaten only on a day when your fat intake in other meals has been below average.

WHAT ABOUT EGG PROTEINS?

Eggs can be used for a variety in the breakfast dishes but these should be restricted to not more than four a week. Latest scientific research shows they are high in cholesterol and if you check with your doctor and find your level of cholesterol is low, you may use eggs more frequently. It is in the yolk of the egg that most of the cholesterol exists. For baking and other cooking purposes eggs should be used. However, replacing the meat proteins with egg proteins is not considered wise and they are not substantial substitutes for the valuable meat proteins.

THE VALUE OF MILK PRODUCTS IN YOUR DIET

It used to be thought that adults did not require milk after their teeth and bones had matured. Now, the latest scientific research shows that milk is really good for everybody, no matter what his age. The only thing that should be avoided by most people is the high cholesterol of the fat in the milk. But today when this fat is removed and we have skimmed milk, or low-fat milk, fortified, we can safely take at least one pint of milk a day. Milk contains many valuable proteins, and when it is used with additional amounts of Vitamins A and D that fortify the milk, it becomes a highly nutritious food. You can also take buttermilk occasionally to add variety.

A very good, quick way to build energy when you feel a sense of fatigue, due to lowered blood sugar, is to fortify a glass of skimmed milk with two tablespoonfuls of dried milk. This enriches the skimmed milk and makes it more palatable.

You can also use yogurt that is made from non-fat milk and it adds to the body's nutrition without giving you too many fat-calories. However, it must be remembered that yogurt is assimilated easily without much work for the stomach and all such foods add more calories than those that the stomach has to work harder to digest. So do not feel you can eat all the yogurt you want, without adding some fattening calories.

WHAT ABOUT CHEESE PRODUCTS?

There are few cheeses that fit in any sustaining diet if they are eaten in large quantities, for most cheeses are high in butterfat content. This includes cheese dips and cheese spreads of all kinds. If you are at a party however, and these are served, you can safely eat a few if you have restricted your high-calorie foods for that day in other departments.

Cottage cheese or pot cheese can be used in your sustaining diet if it is made from non-fat milk. Most cottage cheese must contain a certain amount of butterfat to meet federal regulations. Check your brand of cottage cheese to be sure that it does not contain excessive amounts of butterfat. Many people make this error in dieting—they eat all the cottage cheese they want, never knowing that unless it is the low butterfat type of cottage cheese it is NOT a real good food for losing weight.

THE VALUE OF VEGETABLES IN THE MAINTENANCE DIET

The list of vegetables given for the vegetable soup and the power-pack reducing vegetables may all be eaten in any sustaining diet. However, when you want to maintain a well-balanced diet you can also add other vegetables, such as peas, carrots, corn and potatoes.

The ideal way to use vegetables of course, is if they are eaten in nourishing salads raw. If vegetables are cooked in the usual manner by boiling, many of their nutritive elements are destroyed and they are useless to the body. The best way to prepare most vegetables is by steaming them until tender. Cook them with artificial salt, and no oil or fat. Instead of using butter or other fats try using a bouillon cube, or some herbs to add to the taste of the vegetables. Avoid creamed sauces, or heavy butter on your vegetables. If you want to use a little margarine to add to the flavor, heat it and pour it over the steamed vegetables just before serving.

Later, we shall learn how you can be a vegetarian, if you want to adopt a meatless diet, and still not suffer from protein starvation.

FRUITS—NATURE'S SWEET DESSERTS

Many people who go through the rigors of a diet to lose from 10 to 50 pounds complain because most desserts are denied to them while dieting. As a heavy carbohydrate eater misses his sugars, starches and fats more than anything else in his restrictive reducing diet, it is important that your sustaining diet supplies you with some sweets.

Fruits, and desserts made from fruits, are the best way for you to obtain your sugars. As there is no fat in fruits, you never need to worry about cholesterol in a heavy fruit diet. However, if you overeat even of fruits, you will soon find yourself putting the unwanted pounds back on again, for fruits are full of natural sugars, and sugars always put on weight, when taken in excess.

Dates and figs are high in sugars, but make good tasty substitutes for candy and cakes and pies. Prunes are also highly nutritive and fill you up quickly. Eat all the apples, cantaloupes, watermelon and cherries and strawberries you want when they are in season, for these are on the list of fruits that take more calories to digest than they give to your body. Avoid syrups and too much honey, as these are rich in carbohydrates and are converted into fat without much effort by the body.

Eat oranges and pineapples and most other fruits whole, rather than the juices from them, for it takes the stomach longer to digest them and uses up most of the calories in the digestive process. Most fruits can be used while on your sustaining diet without restriction, and they make excellent sources of quick sugar for between-meal snacks.

Tasty fruit salads can be eaten for lunch or dinner. However, it is best to avoid eating citrus fruits when you eat starch foods, such as bread, or corn, or peas. As these two have different chemical digestions, starches and acids should not be eaten at the same meal.

Another good rule to observe is to avoid eating the high protein meats at the same time you eat starches, in breads or vegetables such as corn and peas, or potatoes. Chemical mixtures are not conducive to good digestion when these opposing chemical combinations are eaten in the same meal. This is why many people who are big meat, potato and bread eaters, topping it off with ice cream, cake or pie, often suffer from terrific indigestion and gas attacks later. These foods require different chemicals to digest. Starches digest predominantly in the mouth, whereas proteins digest in the stomach.

WOMAN WITH CHRONIC INDIGESTION CURED

Mabel P. not only was overweight when she first came to see me, but she complained of chronic indigestion. She said doctors had found nothing wrong with her and she accepted this as a cross she had to bear.

In our first consultation I asked her to give me the typical day's food intake she was following. She told me in detail what her diet had been and it was apparent why she suffered from gas, heart burn and chronic indigestion. She was mixing her starches and proteins and acids indiscriminately at all her meals! For instance, at breakfast she took a glass of orange juice, which was fine, but on top of the orange juice she ate a starchy cereal or two eggs with white toast (more starch), and then coffee and cream and sugar. The starches and sugars simply did not mix with the proteins, such as eggs and milk, or with the acids, represented by the orange juice or other citrus fruits.

At lunch she ate more meat; potatoes, white bread (more starch); and sometimes a fruit dessert, or jello with fruit, or sometimes a fruit yogurt. This mixture of fruit acids with starches and proteins made an indigestible combination, as the starches digest predominantly in the mouth, while the meats and fruits digest in the stomach and intestines.

The moment Mabel P. began to eat her proteins and fruits together, and her starches alone, she lost all signs of indigestion! In the morning she drank her orange juice half an hour before her regular meal and she suffered no further discomfort.

SALADS—THE BUFFER FOODS TO KEEP YOU FROM OVEREATING

It is difficult to overeat salads, for they furnish so much bulk that a person can hardly overeat these valuable foods. All kinds of fruits and vegetables may be used in making up salads that will be helpful on your sustaining diet in giving you that satisfied, full feeling, and yet furnishing you with valuable minerals and other elements you require.

Salad dressings are the big danger in reducing as well as in the maintenance diet that follows. It is always wise to avoid the high fat content of the salad dressings on the market and to favor those that are low in fat content. There are many of these salad dressings on the market and they should be used from now on.

In making up your salads be sure to use raw vegetables as much as possible. You can add fresh fruits to appetizing salads, and to fill out your list of salads you might try combining cottage cheese and gelatin. When you cannot get fresh fruits do not be afraid to use canned fruits, being sure you wash off the excess sugar that comes in the thick syrup.

Following are some tasty recipes that utilize salads which can be served for a complete lunch, or added to the dinner menu with meats and other vegetables.

Grapefruit and Asparagus Salad

Use canned asparagus when you cannot obtain it fresh
2 grapefruits
salad greens
1 green pepper

Cut grapefruit into segments, removing all seeds. Put the asparagus stalks on individual plates that have first been prepared with salad greens. Put about 5 or 6 stalks of asparagus on each plate, with the slices of grapefruit arranged to alternate with the asparagus. Cut the green pepper up into slender strips and place a strip alongside the asparagus or across it. Add special reducing dressing and serve.

Coleslaw Salads

Coleslaw prepared in various ways can add a tasty variety to salad menus, especially when prepared with oranges, apples, cucumbers, or pineapple.

To prepare the basic cole slaw, use a slaw cutter or very sharp knife to shred the cabbage. Avoid the tough outer leaves and use the inner tender leaves only. Wash the cabbage thoroughly and after it has been shredded, add minced onion and parsley sprigs, and also 3/4 cup of special low-fat dressing.

To add variety to the above coleslaw recipe add the following ingredients:

Apple Coleslaw: Chop up 2 large apples, without the skin, and cut up 2 pimentos. Add this to the above coleslaw.

Orange Coleslaw: Cut two oranges into segments and then divide them into smaller pieces, and add to the basic coleslaw recipe above.

Pineapple Coleslaw: Remove the onion from the above basic coleslaw and add 1 cup of shredded canned pineapple, or used fresh pineapple if available.

Cucumber Coleslaw: Use 1 large cucumber and chop it up and add to the basic coleslaw.

Apple, Raisin and Walnut Salad

Another good combination for a tasty salad uses apples, raisins and walnuts.

To prepare this salad use a large salad bowl into which you rub a cut clove of garlic, or you may use a half spoon of garlic salt.

Put a teaspoon of mustard in the bowl. Add a tablespoon of salad oil (polyunsaturated oil is preferred to olive oil, although for better taste you may use olive oil). Stir the oil and mustard together, then add 2 tablespoons of lemon juice, and blend all together.

Add fresh cut up lettuce leaves, uncooked garden peas, small cut up carrots, peeled cut up tomatoes, and watercress. Use hard-boiled eggs quartered for garnishing the dish.

To the above basic salad you may add shredded white cabbage, chopped up apples, seedless raisins and chopped up walnuts. Mix with your favorite low-calorie salad dressing and serve.

You may use the above basic salad bowl to prepare a variety of other tasty and nutritious salads.

Bean Sprout Salad

A delicious bean sprout salad can be made as follows:

Use a cupful of bean sprouts, either fresh or canned. Add to this 1/4 cucumber that you dice, 1/2 cup of chutney sauce, and 1 cup of pineapple cubes. Garnish this with sliced tomatoes and halved hard-boiled eggs. You can further decorate the salad bowl with strips of red pimentos or red and green peppers. Add all these ingredients to the basic lettuce salad given previously.

Date, Ginger and Banana Salad

Serve on a bed of lettuce the following ingredients: quartered bananas, cut up lengthwise; dates from which the pit has been removed; and artificial whipped cream dressing, sprinkled lightly with shredded ginger.

Cream Cheese and Pineapple Salad

This is a tasty variety to regular salads and is a complete lunch if served with date nut bread or whole-wheat bread.

Put several pineapple slices on a bed of lettuce, and heap cream cheese on the leaves. Use finely ground nuts over it. No salad dressing is required for this.

Pear, Pepper and Chicory Salad

Serve this in the basic salad bowl given above. Blend chicory pieces and quarters of fresh, ripe pear (or canned), with thin strips of green pepper, and serve on bed of lettuce, with a low-calorie dressing.

Tomato Salads

Stuffed tomato salads are always eye-appealing as well as healthy and nutritious for any sustaining diet.

You can stuff tomatoes with a variety of foods, such as small shrimp, crab, chopped up lobster tails, creamed mushrooms, hard-boiled eggs, cream cheese, chopped nuts, and nut-meat mixtures.

Cut the tops off the ripe tomatoes and take out the center pulp, blending it with the various ingredients given above.

THE USE OF CEREALS IN THE SUSTAINING DIET

Part of the value of any sustaining diet, after the desired weight has been lost, is to add to the future eating habits those foods that give nourishment, variety and necessary nutrients to the future diet, without danger of putting back unwanted pounds that have been lost.

Most cereals are carbohydrates, it is true, but they are also virtually fat free. As some carbohydrates are essential to any balanced, sustaining diet, you can use whole-wheat cereals, bran, cornflakes, oat products such as oatmeal, grits, and hominy, with additions of stewed or canned fruits or fresh fruits like bananas and berries in season. Also prunes, peaches, pears, apricots, figs, dates and raisins may be added for tasty variety to the cereals.

Whole-wheat grains are also important because they contain Vitamin B complex and also proteins. Many people like to add wheat germ to their breakfast cereals. The cereals that are cooked may be cooked with skimmed milk rather than whole milk.

A good solid breakfast is important to any sustaining diet and may include a cereal, cold or hot, with skimmed milk, an egg, poached, or cooked without fat, with bacon, or ham. Fruit, such as orange or grapefruit, berries or other fruits in season, makes for a complete breakfast, with the addition of coffee or tea, using the artificial sugar and real cream.

A GIRL WHO SKIPPED BREAKFASTS
TO REDUCE, SUFFERED FATIGUE

Ruth I. was 24 years of age, and weighed 155 pounds when she began to be serious about losing weight. She had tried drastic reducing methods and sometimes she lost the desired weight but it kept coming back. She tried skipping breakfasts entirely, usually drinking two cups of black coffee, and then having her lunch at the office restaurant, where she was so famished she usually overate on sandwiches and sweets.

When she began the Oriental reducing diet, she suffered from chronic headaches, irritability and nervousness. Her doctor found nothing organically wrong with her, but did tell her she must lose some weight, as her normal weight for her height and age should have been 130 pounds.

The first thing I urged Ruth I. to do in approaching her new Oriental reducing plan was to eat a big breakfast. This amazed her, as she did not realize that lowered blood sugar in the early morning hours often causes symptoms such as she had, and leads to a desire to overeat at lunch.

She ate two eggs, poached, two slices of thoroughly cooked bacon, a slice of whole-wheat toast with butter, and real cream in her coffee. She needed some fats and the cream and butter gave her some of the required daily fat intake she needed to improve her metabolism.

The breakfast she ate kept her from being famished at lunch and she satisfied her protein needs with slices of ham or beef, cheddar cheese, one slice, and a fruit for dessert.

For her dinners Ruth I. had a wide variety of choices according to our Oriental food plan. With rice as the staple, she satisfied her craving for carbohydrates and sugars and soon was tipping the scales at 140 pounds. It took her only three weeks to shed the full 25 pounds and this she did without ever feeling hungry or suffering from the former symptoms of fatigue, irritability and nervousness.

— 10 —

Built-in Safety Features
to Observe in the
7-Day Oriental
Quick Weight Loss Diet

The objections that most physicians and nutritionists have to the usual quick weight loss diets is that they are unbalanced and do not furnish the body with the required vitamins, minerals and other elements that are required to keep the body at its peak of efficiency.

To reassure yourself on that score, you can know that the built-in safety features you can use while on this diet will prevent you from suffering anything negative to your health.

Consider a few facts that have been observed by scientists regarding stringent dietary deficiencies, under forced conditions. Many people who went on hunger strikes of many days were found to suffer from great weight loss but few other physical symptoms. During most of our major wars, when prisoners were put on reduced diets that were close to starvation, it was found that they suffered less from heart disease, high blood pressure and other diseases that usually are thought to be associated with dietary deficiencies. In fact, these prisoners not only suffered from insufficient nourishment, but they were usually in the most unsanitary conditions, they were often tortured and relentlessly questioned, giving added mental stress, and yet they survived these long terms of imprisonment without succumbing to fatal illnesses.

During the period of World War II in Europe, most of the people lacked meats, fats, proteins, vitamins and other foods considered essential to a balanced diet. These thousands upon thousands of people did not collapse from these limitations in their diets. In fact, they seemed to actually become healthier on their reduced diets! They suffered less from diseases of the heart, hypertension, gallbladder disorders and many other diseases that had formerly killed them by the thousands.

During the Nazi invasions of Holland and Norway, when the populations were practically on starvation diets, hospital admissions dropped 40% over periods when the populations were considered well fed and well nourished.

The moment the war ended and people could obtain all the usual killing foods things changed again. By 1949 the rate of heart disease, high blood pressure and other diseases returned to the same statistics as before the war. This proved that people suffer more illnesses from being overfed than from diets where there are some restrictions and limitations over a period of a few weeks.

However, for those who have such fears about reducing diets of any kind, I shall give you some built-in safety features that you may observe during the times you are on the Oriental 7-day reducing plan. You will then be assured of the fact that you are obtaining all the essential vitamins, minerals and other elements that scientists and nutrition experts agree should be in every balanced diet to maintain the body at its peak of health and energy, even during periods of strenuous reducing.

Despite the fact that Americans are considered the best-fed people in the world, most nutrition experts agree that we are able to afford the best food, but that our diets are deficient in most of the important elements of nutrition. If this can occur when we are not dieting to lose weight, how much more can it be said for most reducing diets, that deprive a person of so many foods that are considered essential to a balanced diet?

It is estimated that more than 50 million Americans suffer from disorders due to dietary deficiencies, even when not dieting and on a so-called normal, balanced diet. Some of these disorders include digestive disturbances, constipation, bad teeth, fatigue, skin trouble, nervousness, and many other troublesome disorders.

SUPPLEMENTS TO THE ORIENTAL 7-DAY DIET

To avoid these deficiencies and dangers while on your reducing diet and later, while on the sustaining normal diet, you can begin immediately to add certain vitamins, minerals and other essential elements that are considered vital to good nutrition.

Follow this regime to the letter if you want to gain immeasurable benefits from these dietary supplements while you are on your reducing diet and long after, for the rest of your natural life. These steps will assure you of being fortified with essential protections so you never again will suffer from nutritional deficiencies.

1. Be sure to include each day, in your diet, or in the sustaining diet after you have lost your desired weight, the important B complex vitamins. One capsule generally contains the essential B complexes, but you should check the label or consult with your personal physician to see that you are taking the required amounts of the right vitamins for your personal needs.

The metabolization of carbohydrates requires thiamine or B_1. This also helps break down sugars in the diet to give you energy. Lack of this vitamin produces fatigue, nausea, psychic and emotional disturbances, poor appetite and sometimes sensations of numbness and very often moodiness and depression. Also, lack of this vitamin sometimes produces leg pains.

Also the B complex vitamins include riboflavin, or B_2, niacin, pyridoxine or B_6 and B_{12}.

If these vital elements are lacking in your diet you will have symptoms of every known type of disorder. This vital information is given fully in Chapter 6 of this book, and you should study it carefully again, to be sure you are not missing out on all of these vital vitamins.

2. Daily, use a very important food supplement that has lately been discovered, which is considered to be in the nature of a miracle worker—this is lecithin, which is an extract made from soya beans.

Lecithin can be added to the breakfast cereals, using from two to four tablespoonfuls, which gives you enough of this vital element for the entire day.

Lecithin is a powder that is made by grinding up soya beans. The soya bean was used in the Orient for centuries and only recently have scientists discovered this miraculous substance from the soya bean.

Lecithin plays an important role in the life function of all living cells, in both animals and humans. It is found in all living cells and plays a big part in the body's correct functioning and in its chemistry.

Scientists found that lecithin was helpful in reducing the cholesterol from the blood vessels in the treatment of heart disease. Injections of lecithin in animals were shown to remove the cholesterol plaques that had been deposited in the arteries.

Other experiments with lecithin in the human diet showed other remarkable results: it was found that it helped in the metabolizing of fats; also that it increased the gamma globulin of the blood, which helps resist various infections. They have also found lecithin useful in the prevention and treatments of many diseases including kidney disorders, metabolic disturbances of the skin, such as psoriasis, rheumatic carditis, and diseases of the liver, as well as anemia.

Patients who had been put on this oil-free program of lecithin reported that they felt better in general, had more energy and vitality for their daily work and were sick less than formerly.

A case that I personally had contact with, proving the remarkable powers that lecithin has when added to the human diet, was that of a woman who was 45 years of age, and chronically tired. Brenda W. thought it was a symptom of her change of life and her physician could find nothing organically wrong. She was about 20 pounds overweight when I first met her, and she told me that her sex life with her husband had deteriorated, and she felt no response to his lovemaking and thought there was something wrong with her.

After she had been on the Oriental diet for about two weeks, she lost her desired weight, but still felt no desire for lovemaking with her husband.

It was then that I remembered the remarkable effects that the addition of lecithin to the food plan had on other people and I told her about the results in added sexual vigor as well as untiring energy that these people had known after two or three weeks of taking lecithin and other supplements. She consulted her doctor who told her to try it as she was in good physical condition now and it might help her.

When Brenda reported to me in the next three weeks, I was astounded at the change in her. She walked with a youthful bounce, her eyes were clear and flashed vitality and energy. She told me that after taking about four tablespoonfuls of lecithin powder a day, which she added to her breakfast cereals, she had felt like a youngster again. Her sexual enjoyment came back and she and her husband began a new relationship that promises happiness for the future.

3. Vitamin A and Vitamin C have also been found to be highly beneficial in any diet, used daily. The recommended dosages that have been approved are 25,000 units of Vitamin A and a minimum of 150 mg. of Vitamin C. Many doctors recommended higher dosages and they should be consulted to determine your personal requirements.

4. A few years ago a famous writer on nutrition recommended a standard formula of blackstrap molasses, wheat germ, skimmed milk fortified with powdered milk and yeast as a good daily way to obtain many essential vitamins and minerals. Up to date scientists have often scoffed at this formula but it has not been disproved. It is still considered by many an excellent way in which to obtain essential vitamins and minerals in a natural, easy way.

5. To furnish the body with essential fatty acids which are required in any balanced daily program of nutrition, it is recom-

mended by many doctors that a person take at least two tablespoonfuls of corn oil, safflower or soya bean oil daily. Some people make up salad dressings using these oils, and many people take them with tomato juice to make them more palatabie.

For centuries people in the Far East have known about the value of soybeans in their diet. This is one of the most valuable sources of unsaturated fatty acids and is thought to be one of the reasons why so many Orientals who follow this type of diet have little heart disease and seldom suffer from arteriosclerosis.

Soybean oil can generally be obtained today in the food markets and at health food stores. Each tablespoonful of soya oil contains about 135 calories and it can easily be used in place of olive oil or the other vegetable oils for salads and for various forms of cooking.

6. If you can obtain your vitamins and minerals from natural foods it is better than taking these in capsules and pills, of course. One very good way by which you can obtain many of the essential vitamins and minerals is to grow a trayful of wheat until the sprouts become about two inches high, then pull them up and wash them, adding them to your salads. You can use a tin tray and put sand in it, placing the wheat into the sand, and covering with a damp cloth, giving a little moisture to the seed. In a few days, if you keep the cloth damp, little green shoots will start to come up and when these are one or two inches high you can utilize them as sources of natural vitamins and minerals.

7. Many people are deficient in calcium with its resultant fatigue and other negative effects on the body. To avoid making this mistake, even while dieting, you should take at least two glasses of skimmed milk a day, and add to the milk about two tablespoonfuls of powdered milk. This helps give the body necessary proteins and also keeps the calcium level high. Sometimes, during dieting, you may feel hungry at two or three in the morning, and this may be due to the fact that the blood sugar has reached low levels. It is then that you need something to eat that will raise the blood sugar level but not add extra fat.

You can put three tablespoonfuls of powdered milk into a glass of skimmed milk and drink this. It will begin to give you the extra energy you will require the next morning when you awaken with that down-in-the-mouth feeling, while you are dieting. This is also a good practice to follow even when you are on your regular diet, for this keeps you from growing so hungry that you eat more than you should at regular meals.

Martha N. was a lecture member who tried the Oriental reducing diet with great benefits, shedding about 35 pounds in a period of a little over three weeks. She reported regularly that she felt fine, except that she seemed not to have the energy she had once known when she was younger. She was only 39 years of age, and with the lost weight she should have felt much better.

I remembered research I had done some years ago on calcium deficiency, which scientists had discovered led to fatigue and other negative symptoms. I then told Martha to try adding powdered skimmed milk (with two tablespoonfuls of powdered milk) to her regular diet. She did this between meals, especially in the morning, when she had a very light breakfast. Soon she said she had energy enough to do her regular housework and that the energy lasted until mid-afternoon, when she took another glass of skimmed milk and two more tablespoonfuls of powdered milk. In about three weeks' time Martha N. seemed to be back to normal. She kept up the skimmed milk and powdered milk as a part of her daily supplement, and reported that she had no further trouble with unnatural fatigue.

8. If you carry your lunch to work and are on a diet, you can still keep yourself down to the calories you should absorb by adding some of the following nourishing foods to your lunch without fearing that you are adding weight.

You can carry a 4 oz. serving of any lean meat, and a small container of salad, with a nonfattening dressing.

You can make your sandwiches with a slice of bologna or cooked ham, or any other lean meat, between two slices of Cheddar cheese.

Celery stalks, radishes, and olives add taste to such a lunch and are easy to carry.

You can add hard-boiled eggs and tomatoes to your lunch, without fearing that you are overindulging in fatty foods.

Corned beef slices with lettuce leaves between them also add tasty variety to a luncheon you must eat at work. A fresh apple or orange, or even a fruit compote can be carried along for dessert. Then at dinner you can carry out the balance of your normal Oriental diet with the vegetables or vegetable soup, and the brown rice.

9. You should avoid all alcoholic beverages while on the Oriental diet, for these add many extra calories to your food intake. However, if you have to have a cocktail before dinner or are at a social gathering and you feel you must take a drink, you can add one or two cocktails to your daily intake of calories and cut down on the rice for that day or eat fewer calories in your other foods.

10. One hour of the right kind of exercise can often help you get away with a higher caloric intake in your food. If you have gone on a binge and eaten a piece of pie or cake, which is forbidden on your regular diet, you can burn up these extra calories by vigorous exercise for an hour. You can swim, play tennis, or walk vigorously, or ride a bicycle for an hour and burn up several hundred calories.

11. Of course exercise should be indulged in while you are losing weight as well as throughout your lifetime. If you do simple sitting up exercises a few moments a day you only use up 200 calories an hour—so you cannot eat more just because of this. Exercise has to be vigorous and indulged in daily for an hour or two if you wish to burn up excess calories. Each day walk, swim, play volley ball or tennis, or get some other form of vigorous exercise (being sure to check with your doctor that you have no special condition that forbids such rigorous physical activity) that will ensure you of using up several hundred calories per day. You will lose weight much faster in this way than if you do no physical exercise at all.

A Woman Who Did Not Exercise Weighed 210 Pounds

A woman who came to my lecture work was 210 pounds when she sought me out for an interview. She did not actually come because of her weight—she dismissed that by saying her mother was fat, and it was a hereditary condition, due no doubt, to her glands. This is an excuse that many fat people rely on. What she did come about was the fact that her husband no longer found her attractive, since she had put on all that excess weight, for she had once been only 140 pounds, and with her big frame and height she could carry that quite well. She wanted to know how to bring her husband back to her, as they had been in earlier years.

In studying her personal habits I found that she sat around all day looking at TV, eating snacks in between, which usually included a box of chocolates a week, and other sugar desserts.

In counseling her, I told her first to see her doctor to learn if she could take a stringent diet, and then I remembered in my travels throughout India I had seen one town where the women were extremely fat, from eating large quantities of sweets, which they made. These women weighed from 190 to 250 pounds, and did no exercise but just sat around eating sweets.

Then I recalled other tribes in India where they were physically very active, the men hunting for their meat, the women tending the crops in the fields, and these people were slender, wiry and energetic, with not one fat person in the village.

I had to work very hard to get this woman to give up her sweets, but to win her husband's love back she agreed to do so. Then she was put on the most stringent diet using our Oriental method of vegetables and brown rice, with the stipulation that she was not to sit around all day, but rather indulge in some form of exercise. She joined a woman's reducing gym where she was given exercises that fit her needs, and with this form of physical activity and the Oriental diet combined, she lost 15 pounds the first week. Within three months, she had shed the unwanted pounds and was back to 140 pounds. She reported that she felt better than ever before and her husband's romantic interests had been revived.

— 11 —

How to Add Zest
to Your Oriental Diet
That Brings You
Nourishment Without Fat

Now you are ready to undertake a study of the foods you can add to your Oriental diet that will give zest to your meals without adding fat calories, and which will give you perfect nourishment while you are on the diet and afterwards.

These foods may be eaten after you have taken off the desired number of pounds and your weight is normal. They will give you tremendous energy, keep you young longer and always keep your weight at normal without effort on your part.

The following foods will diversify your Oriental diet and they will be burned up quickly by the body, and not be stored as fat. These vital foods are NOT the carbohydrate foods that put on your weight in the first place, but they are in the protein and fat classification of foods, which give energy but which do not put on the excess fat.

The foods that are in the carbohydrate class, that is, starches and sugars, give joy to the taste buds, for they add pleasure to eating, but they are also the calories that put excess fat on quickly.

The carbohydrate foods are generally high in fat content and are quickly stored by the body as excess fat. These are the well-known desserts, pie, cake, waffles, pancakes, cream sauces, ice cream, cookies and breads.

If you begin now to eliminate most of these excess carbohydrates from your slenderizing diet and never touch them the rest of your life it will help you not only in maintaining your perfect weight, but in being healthier, having more energy, and living longer.

I know you will instantly ask: But aren't carbohydrates considered necessary in the daily diet? To that we can answer: Yes, they are necessary, but only in minute quantities,not in the large amounts most Americans take them in their daily food intake. If you eliminate the above devitalizing carbohydrates and take the Oriental vital list of foods, you will be getting all the carbohydrates you require in your sustaining diet without adding the heavy fat calories represented by starches and sugars.

Breads, potatoes and sweet desserts are the mainstay of the average American diet. You can safely rid your diet of these forever and suffer only one consequence, being healthier and never again growing fat! Yes, the carbohydrate foods are appealing to the taste buds but they are harmful to the body and they put fat on the body that kills.

The Oriental foods, by their wide variety and because they are natural and not devitalized, furnish the body with all the proteins and other elements required to maintain perfect health and keep the body slender and functioning healthfully.

BROWN RICE AND ITS VALUE OVER WHITE RICE

One of the staples in our Oriental diet for reducing without hunger is brown rice. A person may argue that this is a pure carbohydrate food but he would be wrong. Brown rice contains many other vital food elements besides carbohydrates. It is rich in proteins, and in vitamins and minerals. It is only when the natural brown rice has been processed and the coating removed that all the essential vitamins and proteins are removed. However, in the Oriental 7-day reducing diet white rice may be substituted for brown rice (if you cannot get it at your local grocers), for you cannot eat enough of the white rice to put on excess weight. The Chinese, Japanese and Indonesians, as well as three quarters of the world's population who subsist almost entirely on rice are notoriously slender and have vitality and energy without having the usual sicknesses of heart disease, high blood pressure, arthritis and coronary thrombosis.

THE VITAL IMPORTANCE OF THE MEAT PROTEINS

We know that most people in the Orient cannot afford costly beef, lamb and pork, for they do not have the means of feeding large herds of cattle. They often substitute fish as the main staple to a predominantly rice and vegetable diet. However, as I have stated elsewhere, I have amended the Oriental diet to fit our American needs, where we do have an abundance of protein animal foods in a wide and fairly reasonable assortment.

To the filling Oriental staple of brown rice, each day one can add the high protein meats, such as beef, veal, pork and fish, which give a wide variety to the meals as well as assuring one that he will get all the vital proteins he needs, without danger of putting on excess weight.

You can usually eat any meat that you desire to give you the day's necessary proteins, and you will find that your body will not turn it into fat.

Now, obviously, you will not want to eat brown rice every day of your life, for this could become monotonous. You can add rice to the diet three or four times a week, and the rest of the time substitute baked or boiled potatoes, which give you carbohydrates and are not fat-producing, unless fried, or eaten in large quantities.

Besides the high protein beef, veal, lamb, and pork products, you can add to rice and vegetables the other high protein foods of poultry, fish, cheese and eggs. You can get an infinite variety of dishes by using these high protein foods without risking adding extra weight.

Chuck V. was a 215 pound bulldozer operator. His work was not physically strenuous, although it looked as if it was. He sat 8 hours a day and drove the bulldozer, doing no actual physical labor. He was consuming more than 4,000 calories a day, most of it in carbohydrates.

At lunch time Chuck consumed three bread sandwiches, with meat, mayonnaise on the bread, or butter, and a wedge of fruit pie, two cups of coffee with sugar and cream, and at home he ate meat, bread, potatoes, coffee, usually had a couple of beers while watching TV and just before going to bed, he would have a dish of ice cream or pie or cake, or both. No wonder this man, who was only 30 years of age, was gaining weight and could not seem to stop it.

It was difficult for Chuck to eat the reducing soup and he did not like vegetables, so to get him on a reducing diet was difficult, as he was afraid he would be perpetually hungry and not have enough energy to do his day's work.

In this instance I told Chuck he could eat all the lean meat he desired at lunch, breakfast, and dinner, but he must cut out all bread and butter, pies and cakes and other sweets. He was to add the brown rice three times a day, with the lean meat, and drink his coffee with artificial sugar and cream, the non-dairy kind. In between meals he had been drinking quantities of cokes and soft drinks, with sugar. I told him he could drink the dietetic, sugar-free type of cokes and this would kill his appetite for sweets.

He carried cheese and bologna sandwiches, with the cheese between slices of bologna, for his lunch, and fresh fruit for dessert. Chuck consumed more food than ever in this way but he had cut down so much on the carbohydrate calories that he began to lose weight steadily and in three months' time he was down to his normal 175 pounds.

Here is a list of the wide varieties of high protein meats that are available for your future diet, which assure you that you will have variety and highly nutritional protein for the rest of your life, without putting on excess weight, if you eat a normal portion once a day.

HIGH PROTEIN FOODS YOU CAN SAFELY USE
AND HOW TO PREPARE THEM

Chuck and round steak	Roast or broil in oven
Chopped ground steak	Broil or fry without fat
Porterhouse steak	Broil
T-Bone steak	Broil
Tenderloin steak	Broil
Prime ribs of beef	Roast
Sirloin of beef	Roast
Filet mignon	Broil
Short ribs	Brown and broil
Sweetbreads	Fry
Liver	Broil or fry without fat
Kidney	Broil
Heart	Stew
Brains	Fry with cooking oil or butter

LAMB

Leg of lamb	Roast in oven
Chopped lamb patties	Broil
Breast of lamb	Roast
Rack of lamb	Roast
Lamb chops	Broil

PORK PRODUCTS

A word of caution regarding pork products: Even when you are not reducing it is good to limit the consumption of pork to a minimum. It can add taste and variety to your usual routine diet but all pork products are high in fat and these are rich foods, high in calories. Now, it is true your body does require some fats, but only about 45 to 60 grams a day, whereas most Americans consume as high as 450 grams of high-calorie, fat foods per day. Even a laborer does not need that many fat calories a day.

Fresh ham	Boil or roast
Smoked ham	Bake or fry
Bacon	Broil or fry
Loin of pork	Roast
Spareribs	Broil or fry
Shoulder of pork	Bake
Pork chops	Bake or fry

VEAL PRODUCTS

Veal cutlets	Fry
Veal steaks	Broil
Round	Roast

POULTRY

Chicken	Roast, broiled or fried
Turkey	Roast
Pheasant	Roast or broil
Squab	Roast
Goose (high in fat)	Roast
Duckling (also high in fat)	Roast
Guinea hen	Roast

OTHER PROTEIN MEAT PRODUCTS

Frankfurters	Boil or broil in oven
Bologna	No cooking needed
Liverwurst	Ready to eat
Salami	Ready to eat
Knockwurst	Boil or fry

A word of caution regarding the proteins given above: These are usually to be eaten with caution, even when you are not reducing, for most of them are high in fat content and they are processed meats that are not as nutritious as fresh meats. They are good to use as luncheon meats in sandwiches or for special occasions, but are not recommended as a steady diet.

FISH FOODS

Halibut	Broil or bake
Salmon, fresh	Bake or poach
Salmon, canned	Ready to eat
Mackerel	Broil or bake
Trout	Broil, bake, or fry
Tuna, canned	Ready to eat
Codfish	Broil or bake
Haddock	Broil or bake
Swordfish	Broil, bake or fry
Perch	Broil, bake or fry
Whitefish	Bake or broil
Lobster	Broil
Shrimp	Boil or fry
Crab	Boil or fry
Mussels	Steam
Scallops	Broil or fry
Clams	Bake, fry, or raw
Oysters	Fry, bake, or raw

CHEESE PRODUCTS

Many nutritionists recommend cheese products as good meat substitutes in a diet, but most cheese products are filled with salt and require a great deal of drinking of water. This water is retained by the body cells and often can add as much as ten to fifteen pounds of bloat and weight.

Cheeses should be used sparingly. Cottage cheese, yogurt and pot cheese are good sources of proteins and should be used often.

Whole milk can be used by those who need extra fat in their diets, but most adults can easily use skimmed milk without the danger of extra fat, and this furnishes valuable proteins and other minerals and vitamins without furnishing the body with extra fat calories that it does not need.

Eggs can safely be used in most diets as a valuable form of protein, but because of the high cholesterol content of the egg yolk most nutritionists recommend limiting the number of eggs to four a week. However, you should check your own personal cholesterol level with your doctor and if he finds that it is low, he may recommend that you can eat more of this high cholesterol food.

Eggs can be poached, scrambled, fried, and boiled. They add variety to breakfast menus and are tasty in salads.

Try eggs prepared in the following ways to add variety to your breakfasts.

Eggs Benedict

Prepare three or four pieces of toast, depending on the number of people you will have at breakfast. Slightly cook slices of ham in margarine. Poach your eggs, and then place the slices of ham on the toast, with a poached egg on each and put hollandaise sauce on top. This makes a tasty dish and is a good variety for the usual boring breakfasts.

There are many wonderful omelets that are easy to prepare and which add variety. Beat the desired number of eggs in a bowl, and put them into a non-sticking pan over moderate heat. Let the eggs firm on the bottom, and while still not cooked on top, put in the filler you want for the omelet.

You can use chopped mushrooms (which should be slightly cooked before adding to the eggs). You can also use chicken livers, (also pre-cooked before adding to the eggs). You can use onions and green peppers and also jelly. You can invent other interesting fillers if you are skillful.

Breakfast can be given added zest by preparing your eggs with cut up pieces of bacon in a frying pan, and then putting eggs on top and shirring them. You put them into a baking dish and bake for about 10 minutes in the oven. You can also add variety by using chicken livers, pieces of cooked sausage, or Canadian bacon in the shirred eggs.

Do not be afraid to add meats to your breakfast dishes, or you can sometimes add fish, or cheese. A cheese omelet is easy to prepare and is nutritious and tasty. Use Cheddar cheese for an omelet, and fold the cut up pieces of cheese into the omelet when it is cooked firm on the bottom.

If you must eat sandwiches, use the whole-wheat breads and toast them. Use only one slice of bread for the sandwich, rather than two. You can use ham, bologna, tuna fish, tongue, chicken salad or cold chicken or turkey, and serve with it a dish of cole slaw, or tomatoes. A sandwich with pickles or relish, and a bowl of low-fat soup, such as split pea, lentil or bean soup, makes a filling lunch, if the bread is cut down to only one slice.

KEEP VEGETABLES HIGH ON THE LIST OF FOODS TO EAT

With your protein needs adequately provided for in your future diets, do not forget to add a wide variety of vegetables that are essential to a well-balanced diet. You can now safely include some of the higher-calorie vegetables, which were forbidden when you were on the quick weight loss diet.

You can now expand your list of fresh and cooked vegetables to include the starchier ones such as peas, carrots and beans. Lima beans are a good staple food for they not only contain valuable proteins, but have sufficient carbohydrates to satisfy the body's requirements. Navy beans are also excellent for this source—they can be baked, or made into a tasty soup by adding a couple of onions chopped up, and a tablespoonful of tomato paste.

The following list of vegetables may be consulted for adding variety to your daily intake of these valuable foods.

Beets	Okra
Carrots	Green Peppers
Chard leaves	Tomatoes
Green string beans	Egg Plant
Green peas (fresh if possible, or canned if not)	Spinach
	Lettuce
Corn	Watercress
Kale	Broccoli
Turnips	Asparagus
Mustard greens	Brussel sprouts
Squash	Cucumbers
Artichokes	Leeks
Celery	Onions
Escarole	Garlic
Cabbage	Radishes

WIDE VARIETY OF FRESH FRUITS IN SEASON

To give you the valuable natural sugars for energy, do not neglect the fruits that are in season to give you the balanced nutrition that is so essential to good health

Among these fruits are:

Apples	Watermelon
Apricots	Cantaloupe
Cherries	Oranges
Strawberries	Grapefruit
Pears	Lemons
Peaches	Tangerines
Grapes	Bananas

The following list of foods represents most of the high-calorie, fattening foods which should be used sparingly. You can substitute fruits, figs, dates and nuts for satisfying the carbohydrate urge that makes people eat so many of the forbidden foods.

Avoid these foods, especially in large quantities:

Avocado	Marmalade
Bacon (unless fat is cooked out)	Syrup
	Waffles
Cakes	Pancakes
Pies	Hominy
Ice cream	Jelly
Candy (unless it is health candy with artificial sugar)	Macaroni
	Spaghetti
Chocolate	Noodles
Cocoanut	Olive Oil
Crackers	Peanut butter
Doughnuts	Popcorn
French dressing or other rich dressings (use diet dressings only)	Potatoes
	Pretzels
	Puddings (unless you use the sugar free puddings)
All fried foods	Sour cream
Gravy	
Honey	

USE RAW VEGETABLES WHENEVER POSSIBLE

Most of the valuable elements are cooked out of vegetables by the American housewife. The water that is used to cook most vegetables should be saved and used to make gravies (without the addition of fat), or soups. Vegetables are best cooked when slightly steamed, until tender enough to pass a fork through them, with as little water as possible.

But as many raw vegetables as possible should be used as

salads. Here are some combinations that are tasty and nutritious without being fattening.

Add fresh green lima beans and kernels of corn with raw vegetable salad of lettuce, cucumbers, tomatoes and green peppers. Use a low-calorie French or Russian dressing.

Make a salad of shredded lettuce, spinach leaves chopped up, and watercress. Add tomatoes and cucumbers, and serve with a small portion of cottage cheese or pot cheese, with your favorite salad dressing (the low-calorie variety which can be found on the market shelves or which you can make yourself).

Another good combination of salads is lettuce, chopped up celery, spinach leaves, and chopped up tomatoes. Use a dressing of lemon and garlic.

A salad can be made with carrots finely chopped, raw cabbage, and raw beets with greens, finely chopped. Serve with a low-calorie dressing as a luncheon salad with a fish dish.

An avocado salad is high in calories but if you have been sparing in your fat intake, you can chop up an avocado, celery, green pepper, onion, and serve on a bed of cut up lettuce. Use a ripe avocado. Use a low-calorie Roquefort or Russian dressing.

SAUCES AND LOW-CALORIE SALAD DRESSINGS TO USE WITH THE ORIENTAL REDUCING DIET

Many times meats and salads can be given taste-appeal by using sauces and low-calorie salad dressings which keep you from feeling you are dieting.

Many wonderful sauces can be made by using some of the following ingredients: ketchup, tomato puree, wine or wine vinegar, Worcester sauce, and anchovy essence. Use dried herbs, pepper, artificial salt and other seasonings like garlic powder to add zest to your vegetables, meats and salads.

French Dressing

Make enough to fill a large bottle—it will keep indefinitely.

1 cup of tomato juice
1/4 tsp. garlic powder
1 cup wine vinegar or tarragon vinegar

1/2 tsp. dry mustard
1/2 tsp. oregano
a touch of artificial sugar
artificial salt to taste
a touch of black pepper

Combine the above ingredients in a glass jar and shake thoroughly before using. Store in refrigerator.

Sour Cream Sauce

2 cups of diet cottage cheese
1/2 teaspoon lemon juice
1/2 cup buttermilk
artificial salt

This can be used over fresh vegetable salads, or even fruits.

Horseradish Sauce

This is good to serve with lean meats or for various types of fish.

Use the sour cream recipe given above and add to this 2 tbs. of white or red horseradish.

Sauce Vinaigrette

2 cloves of minced or diced garlic
4 tbs. water
1 tsp. herbs (tarragon, rosemary, thyme, dill)
1/4 tsp. paprika
touch of artificial sweetener

Shake together in closed jar and keep in refrigerator.

Cheese Sauce

1/2 cup of buttermilk
1/2 pound farmer cheese
1 egg yolk
1/2 tsp. paprika
2 tbs. lemon juice
salt and pepper to taste

Use a double boiler to prepare this sauce. Melt the cheese and buttermilk, then put in the egg yolk and blend thoroughly. Add the paprika, salt, pepper and lemon juice. This is an excellent sauce and can be used over vegetables of all kinds.

Yogurt Dressing

>1 clove of diced garlic
>1/2 cup celery leaves
>1 tsp. salt
>2 tbs. tomato paste
>2 cups yogurt (plain)
>1 cup of diced onions
>sweeten to taste with artificial sugar

Mix thoroughly in an electric blender until smooth. It is excellent as a dressing for green salads. (Makes about 3 cups.)

Meat Sauce, Marinade

All lean meats that are intended to be broiled, such as steaks, shish kebab, lamb, etc. can first be prepared with this marinade sauce and kept in the ice box wrapped in a plastic bag for at least overnight. It helps give the meats a delicious flavor.

>2 cups of dry red wine
>2 tsp. salt
>2 tsp. mustard (dry)
>2 bay leaves
>6 cloves
>2 sliced onions
>2 cloves of garlic, minced
>2 stalks celery, chopped
>2 cups tarragon vinegar
>6 peppercorns

If the above amounts are excessive, store in a glass jar in the refrigerator and use another time.

Low-Calorie Salad Dressing

>3 cups of skimmed milk
>2 tsp. mustard
>4 tbs. cornstarch
>2 egg yolks
>1/2 cup lemon juice
>1 tsp. salt substitute

Blend the milk and cornstarch in a double boiler, and heat it until it makes a smooth paste. Mix together the egg yolks, mustard, salt and lemon juice in a separate bowl. When the milk and cornstarch are a smooth paste over low flame, add the egg mixture to this, until it thickens, and then put into a jar and cool. It can be kept in the refrigerator and used when wanted.

Tasty French Dressing

    2 cups of canned tomato juice
    2 tbs. cornstarch
    4 tbs. salad oil
    1/2 cup vinegar
    1/2 tsp. paprika
    1/2 tsp. horseradish
    1/2 tsp. onion salt
    1/2 tsp. celery salt
    1 tsp. Worcester sauce
    1/2 tsp. dry mustard
    1/2 tsp. garlic powder

Use 1 cup of water in a pan and add cornstarch; stir until it forms a smooth paste. Then add the tomato juice and cook, stirring it, until it is thick. Then cool it and add the other ingredients, beating it until smooth. Store in a refrigerator and use as needed.

Blue Cheese Dressing

    1 container of cottage cheese
    4 tbs. vinegar
    4 tbs. water
    2 8-oz. envelopes of blue cheese salad dressing mix (or you may chip up
        blue cheese or Roquefort chunks if you prefer)

Blend the above ingredients in an electric blender, and store in a glass jar in the refrigerator. Double the above quantities if you wish to make up a larger portion to last for longer periods.

Salad Dressing a la Creme

For this you can use the excellent creamy style salad dressings found in markets in tin foil envelopes.

1 cup of tomato juice
4 tbs. vinegar
2 envelopes of salad dressing mix

Mix above in bowl with 4 tbs. of water, and store in a glass jar in the refrigerator.

Hollandaise Sauce

2 tbs. cream
1/2 tsp. salt
4 egg yolks
touch of Cayenne pepper
1/2 cup butter or margarine
1/2 tsp. dry mustard

Put a bowl in a pan of hot water and mix egg yolks, vinegar, cream, salt and pepper together in bowl. Put over moderate heat and beat with an egg beater. Do not boil water, but let it become hot. Add margarine or butter when the mixture begins to thicken, beating it until butter melts.

This sauce is delicious over broccoli, green beans, and asparagus. Also excellent to serve over eggs Benedict.

Your Own Low-Calorie Mayonnaise

4 egg yolks   1/2 tsp. white pepper
2 tsp. salt   1/2 cup lemon juice
1/2 tsp. paprika   2 1/2 cups salad oil
2 tsp. dry mustard

In a bowl combine the lemon juice, egg yolks and seasonings. Stir with a rotary beater while adding salad oil slowly, about 1 tablespoon at a time, until all oil has been used. Add another tablespoon of lemon juice while adding the balance of salad oil, and beat until it is thick. Store in refrigerator.

— 12 —

How to Extend
the 7-Day Oriental Diet
if You Want to Lose
More Than Twenty Pounds

Perhaps you come in the category of people who feel that a weight loss of ten or fifteen pounds is not enough and you want to continue on this Oriental diet to shed from 20 to 50 more pounds safely and without hunger or effort.

You can easily do this by following the basic principles of the Oriental quick weight loss diets given elsewhere, and adding to them the combinations and variations which follow. The purpose of this is to give a wide variety of foods to those who are forced to go beyond the one or two week periods that most people require to shed only a few pounds. This can be done in a wide variety of ways and by adding low-calorie foods that will keep you perfectly nourished while at the same time melting away the unwanted pounds.

VARIATION DIETS FOR THOSE WANTING
TO LOSE MORE THAN 20 POUNDS

Many times people want to lose more than 20 pounds and they have to use the Oriental reducing diet for a period of three or four weeks beyond the 7-day period. The following variation diets may be used to add variety to the diet and also to give more balanced nutrition. The monotony of using only rice or vegetables, or a combination of these for several weeks, usually discourages people from continuing long enough to shed the additional pounds when they weigh 200 or more pounds.

Woman Lost 100 Pounds on Extended Oriental Diet

There was one woman, Mrs. Bernice R., who had a difficult weight problem. When she started the Oriental food and diet plan she weighed 250 pounds. She was chronically fatigued, had nervous headaches, high blood pressure, erratic heart action and was a chronic asthmatic. Her doctors had despaired of her ever losing weight, for she had tried every known diet, all without success. She would lose as much as ten or fifteen pounds and then go off the diet wagon, and gain it right back.

Of course Mrs. R. fell back on the usual excuse when she first came to me out of desperation to help her. "It must be my glands!" she moaned as she fell into a large chair. "My mother was heavy all her life. It seems to run in the family, at least on the women's side."

I explained to Mrs. R. that usually when the mother is fat, the children also become heavy, owing to the fact that they are all on the same diet . . . usually a heavy sugar, starch, and carbohydrate diet that sets the eating habits of a youngster early in life. I did not accept the glandular excuse that most people use as a crutch to explain their obesity.

Mrs. R. began with the two day fasting period, and immediately had high hopes when she saw she had lost five pounds. Of course, this was excess water she had accumulated in her tissues, but it gave her courage to continue the Oriental diet.

After two weeks on the stringent diet of only vegetables and brown rice, she had shed another 25 pounds, but she was terribly tired of the monotony of being denied other foods. It was then that she went on the extended variation diets, for I could see she would have to vary the diet if she was to remain on it and shed another 70 pounds. I estimated that she could easily get rid of about 10 pounds a week, which would take her seven more weeks of sticking with the diet. These diet variations are given on the following pages if you should need them in your case.

I put her on the vegetable and meat diet for the third week of the diet, and she registered 12 pounds less at the end of the week.

The next week she went on the fish and tomato diet, which allowed her to eat any kind of fish, such as bass, tuna, salmon, shrimp, lobster, halibut, abalone, or flounder, broiled, and two medium sized tomatoes at each meal. She could eat tomatoes between meals also.

Then Mrs. R. started the lean meat and tomato regimen for the next week, and again showed a loss of 12 pounds.

The next week she ate all the vegetables she wanted on the desired list which follows, and this gave her three or four vegetables a day, and as these were the reducing vegetables, she was able to continue losing even when she stuffed herself on the high power reducing vegetables.

For one full week she went on the low-calorie reducing fruits, eating all she wanted of watermelon, cantaloupe, apples, and pumpkin, and in that one week she was able to rid herself of 15 more pounds. The reason for the quicker weight loss on fruits was that these fruits all require more calories to digest than they give to the body. Naturally, she could not continue on such a stringent diet indefinitely, without harm to her health, but for only one week it did no harm. She drank eight to ten glasses of water a day, and as the body was not receiving any fat whatsoever on this diet, it was being forced to burn up its own fat! This was one reason why she was able to lose the 100 pounds in such a short space of time. As she had to have some other variations to the diet for such a long period of time, she began to eat some boiled eggs or cottage cheese with her fruits and vegetables, and also skimmed milk—two glasses a day fortified with two tablespoonfuls of powdered dry milk.

I observed Mrs. R. over a period of many months after she

had completed her strenuous reducing and I am happy to report that periodic checkups with her personal doctor while she dieted and afterwards revealed that many of her physical symptoms began to disappear with the fat, and today, she is down to her desired weight of about 150 pounds.

FISH AND TOMATO DIET

For one entire week, during the four weeks or more of the Oriental diet, use the Fish and Tomato only plan. Each day you may eat half a pound of delicious broiled fish. This can be eaten three times a day! You need not worry about putting on too many calories on this diet and it is excellent for fish lovers. In other words, you are actually eating 1 1/2 pounds of fish on this diet, enough to more than satisfy your protein needs. You do not add any carbohydrates, sugars or starches. You do not add vegetables, or even rice on this variation plan. During that week you will probably tire of this fish diet and you will then want to go on to another of our variation Oriental diets, where you can still continue to lose five to seven pounds a week until the desired weight has been achieved.

You may select any of the following types of fish:

Tuna (canned or fresh)	Flounder
Sea bass	Halibut
Cod steaks	Salmon
Shrimp	Abalone
Lobster	Shad Roe
Oysters	

You can use three varieties of fish on any one day, which gives you a wide variety without tiring your taste buds. For breakfast you can use creamed tuna on a piece of whole-wheat toast, rather than cereal or eggs. It is an excellent protein substitute and will not endanger the caloric intake.

THE SECOND WEEK YOU MIGHT
TRY MEAT AND TOMATOES ONLY

I have personally seen many people drop pounds of excess weight using only meat and tomatoes. You can eat half a pound of any lean meat three times a day, which gives a total intake of 1 1/2 pounds of this protein food. Drink plenty of water on this Meat and Tomatoes diet, for it is helpful in flushing out all the excess acid ash, and uric acid that a great deal of meat gives the body. You can eat three tomatoes a day, raw or canned, and this diet will give you a perpetually full feeling without that strong craving most dieters have for starches and sugars.

Some of the low-calorie meats you may use on this diet are:

Filet mignon
Ground lean meat (broiled or fried without fat)
Liver (broiled)
T-Bone steak
Sirloin steak
Tenderloin steak
Lamb chops or breast of lamb
Veal
Pork chops (broiled, with fat removed)
Pot roast
Sweetbreads

A good variation breakfast while you are on your meat and tomatoes diet is to have broiled kidneys on toast—or sweetbreads on toast, or chipped beef on whole-wheat toast.

This meat and tomatoes diet is a rich variation to the usual reducing plans given in this book, and is not to be encouraged as a steady diet, for it is essential that vegetables, fruits, some carbohydrates and fats be added to the regular sustaining diets. It must be used only as a means for achieving variety to the monotony of the usual reducing diets.

ALL VEGETABLE DIET

A wonderful variation to the regular Oriental 7-day diet for one week is an all vegetable diet, which gives you a complete list of vegetables which will never add weight, but which will furnish you with most of the body's nutritive elements.

There are certain vegetables which are higher in calories than others and these should be avoided for the one week vegetable diet. The forbidden vegetables are:

Avocados
Beans (white)
Lentils
Sweet potatoes
Corn

You can eat several meals just of vegetables, as many as 6 meals a day, without worrying about adding too many calories. In fact, some people who choose to be vegetarians live on nothing but vegetables, with some milk products, eggs, nuts and grains, and occasionally fish. They never eat red-blooded meat of any kind and these people remain remarkably slender and seem to have tremendous energy and vitality. However, I do not recommend a complete vegetarian diet unless you have carefully checked with your doctor to see that there are no special conditions in your case which require greater variation in your food intake.

You may select a wide variety of vegetables from the following list and vary them from day to day, eating as much as you want for each meal. Your capacity is limited when it comes to vegetables so it becomes impossible to overeat. The following vegetables furnish the body with fewer calories than others, and require more calories to digest than they give to the body.

Tomatoes	Broccoli	Mushrooms
Turnips	Cabbage	Sauerkraut
Lettuce	Brussel Sprouts	Cauliflower
Green Peppers	Celery	Leeks
Radishes	Asparagus	Kohlrabi
Cucumbers	String Beans	Garlic
Watercress	Spinach	Okra

The following vegetables may be added if you continue the vegetable diet beyond the first week, although these have more fat-calories than the above list of vegetables.

Beets	Squash
Carrots	Rutabagas
Kale	Parsnips
Onions	Chives
Red Peppers	Artichokes
Parsnips	

The vegetables can be steamed until soft, and then to add some flavor you may use a little melted butter or margarine. The fat butter calories will be tolerated on this strict diet, as there are no other forms of fat or starches in this diet.

You can eat as many varieties of vegetables each day as you wish, using about 1 cup of each per day. You might select several vegetables one day and others the next day, giving a variety so you do not tire of them. You could eat as many as 15 cups of these vegetables a day, in addition to a large fresh tomato and a head of lettuce, with a low-calorie dressing, and you would hardly exceed 900 calories per day.

However, if you begin to add other foods and high calorie dressings on the raw vegetable salads, you soon will have several hundred more calories, that will be fat-calories that put your weight back on quickly.

You can use herbs, spices, and low-calorie dressings to give taste variety to your vegetables. You can also eat a large baked potato with margarine for the evening meal but you should avoid all eggs, cheeses, creams, bread, nuts, milk and other foods that would tend to unbalance this vegetable diet.

However, if you should decide to choose the lacto-vegetarian diet as a sustaining diet for the remainder of your life, you may safely add some butter, cheese, including cottage cheese and pot cheese, yogurt, nuts, grains, and rice, and you can be assured that you will never again have a weight problem. This natural diet of natural foods is the nearest thing to our pure Oriental food plan, for remember, most people in the eastern countries cannot eat meat, as it is prohibitive, and many are forbidden to eat the flesh of animals by their religions, so they exist entirely on the lacto-vegetarian foods given above.

ETERNALLY YOUNG GLORIA SWANSON
AND HER DIETARY KNOW-HOW

Some years ago, when I was known as the adviser to the Hollywood stars, I had a radio program on the Don Lee Mutual

Network, and Gloria Swanson was my guest. I was delighted to find out in the several days we spent together going over the notes for our program that the glamorous movie star knew more about health and diet than most nutrition experts.

When we had lunch and she saw what I ordered (for in those days, being younger, I was not too concerned about my diet or weight) Gloria remarked, "That is not a well-balanced diet." Then I observed what she ordered and I realized why she had such a slender figure and why she has retained it throughout the years. Gloria ordered a tossed green salad with watercress, lettuce, cut up green pepper, cucumbers, minced onions and a dressing which she mixed at the table, consisting of lemon juice and two tablespoonfuls of olive oil.

For her main course she ordered a cheese dish made with mushrooms, and she ate no meat at lunch. I do not think she has ever been a heavy meat eater, for in talking to her I found she was a great believer in natural foods, grains, vegetables, milk products, with fat removed, and all kinds of fruits. We discussed vegetable and fruit juices, and she was a firm believer that these were nature's ways for flushing out the body's acids and alkalinizing the body, preventing disease.

I have seen Gloria Swanson at parties, where rich foods and drinks were served, and I never observed her drinking or smoking, and she nibbled on vegetables, salads, and fruits. She has kept her youth and her slender figure throughout the years because of her careful habits in eating only natural foods.

THE REDUCING POWER OF FRUITS ONLY

You may achieve more rapid weight loss on an all fruit diet than even on the all vegetable diet, and it is much more palatable to your taste buds, as well as highly nutritious. You can start your fruit diet with breakfast, and then eat at least six or seven times a day, and never fear that you are overdoing.

There are two categories of fruits which you may use in the all fruit reducing plan. The first one includes those fruits that require more calories to digest than they give to the body. The ones on the other list add some calories. These two groups may be intermingled, so you can select some fruits from the first list and add a few from the second list.

However, if your aim is a complete loss of several pounds you should stick to the list of low-calorie fruits given in List No. 1.

List No. 1—The Low-Calorie Reducing Fruits

Cantaloupe
Pumpkin
Honeydew melon
Watermelon
Rhubarb

List No. 2—The Higher-Calorie Fruits

Peaches	Apples	Oranges
Pears '	Cherries	Cranberries
Blackberries	Grapes	Nectarines
Apricots	Grapefruit	Papaya
Lemons	Pineapples	Raspberries
Limes	Plums	Fresh strawberries
Loganberries	Prunes (fresh)	Tangerines

Should you eat canned fruits on this all fruit diet? Only if fresh fruits are not available or in season. Then you should select brands that are packed in low-calorie, sugar free syrup, found on the shelves of dietetic foods in your grocery store. If you use regular canned fruits in heavy syrup be sure to wash off the syrup.

If you wish to continue your all fruit diet into the second or third weeks, and you continue to lose from 5 to 10 pounds a week, you may add interesting variations with the addition of other foods, such as cottage cheese, boiled eggs, vegetables, yogurt and skimmed milk.

You may also use a variation that many people like, which continues to give them weight loss, and at the same time satisfies their taste buds with a delicious variety. This is a combination of fruits and vegetables taken from the above lists. Mix two or more vegetables and fruits from the above lists, and eat at least four or five times a day, or whenever you are hungry. You need not bother counting calories in this diet for you can seldom eat more than 900 or 1000 calories a day on this fruit and vegetable diet.

After consuming a few cupfuls of fruits and vegetables, you will have a comfortably full feeling. Then add several glasses of water per day, at least 8, and you will never have that hungry, gnawing feeling that comes when you are on the usual diet.

Bananas are not given in the above lists of fruits for an obvious reason—they are highly placed in the carbohydrate list of foods. However, if you have a craving for bananas, you can try an all banana and skimmed milk diet for one week, and you will find you will still continue to lose weight and at the same time indulge your craving for starches and carbohydrates. Each banana contains about 85 calories, and skimmed milk per glass is about 90 calories. You can alternate your bananas and skimmed milk, and eat as many as 8 good sized bananas and 8 glasses of skimmed milk a day, and not consume more than 900 to 1000 calories a day.

HOW JOAN CRAWFORD USES THESE REDUCING TECHNIQUES

Several years ago, when I was doing a series of lectures in Honolulu, I was walking through the International Market Place, and ran into an old friend, whom I have known for many years, Joan Crawford. We had lunch at the Royal Hawaiian Hotel, where she was staying, and talked over old days, when she was one of Hollywood's most glamorous stars and I had advised her on many aspects of her career.

Joan admitted she had occasionally had a weight problem over the years, and she had to be careful, as we all should be, of her diet, so she could keep up her energy and still retain her youthful figure and her good health. As an executive for the Pepsi-Cola company, and also in her strenuous hours before the cameras in her still-successful screen career, Joan told me she had to carefully choose foods that would give a maximum amount of energy without adding weight.

I was interested to see what she would order for luncheon in the glamorous setting of palm trees and hibiscus blossoms surrounding the Royal Hawaiian hotel.

Joan ordered papaya halves filled with cottage cheese, and then a bowl of fresh fruits, including slices of pineapple, honeydew melon, cantaloupe and watermelon. She said "I seldom eat a heavy lunch, but I always include some kind of fruit in a salad or by itself. When I am at the studio working, I keep a bowl of fresh in-season fruits in my dressing room all day, and when I am hungry, I nibble on fruit. This satisfies my craving for sugar and gives natural sugar energy without adding any fat to the body."

During lunch we talked about diet and health and I found that the glamorous star had observed a dietary plan all through the years, which was similar to my own, and which I have called the Oriental reducing diet. For keeping her weight at normal, Joan told me she eats a small portion of lean meat at dinner, usually chicken, fish, a steak, or broiled calf's liver, with two generous helpings of green or yellow vegetables, and her dessert is usually fruit, or a thin slice of cheese. She has the boundless energy and enthusiasm of a young girl, and I believe this is due to the fact that she has observed these strict dietary rules all her life. I asked her about rice, and she told me she includes it in her menus at least twice a week, instead of the usual staple, potatoes.

BANANAS AND SKIMMED MILK
RID HIM OF 25 UNWANTED POUNDS

Burt E. weighed 210 pounds when he started his Oriental reducing diet, and he kept at it faithfully for the first two weeks, getting rid of 15 pounds a week. But then he got tired of the monotony of the diet and wanted a change of pace, so I suggested he try the bananas and skimmed milk diet, eating about 8 bananas a day and drinking at least 8 glasses of skimmed milk per day. This was a pleasant variety to his diet, as he liked bananas, and he was able to keep this up for one week, without monotony. He lost only 10 pounds that week, but as he now weighed 170 pounds, which was about normal for him, he went on the sustaining diet, and kept his weight at that level in the months I observed him. He was an office worker and it was no great difficulty for him to reduce his caloric intake to less than 1000 calories during the several weeks he needed to shed his weight.

ALTERNATING DIETS

You might try alternating your fruit, vegetable and banana days as follows:

One day use the all fruit diet.
The second day use the all vegetable diet.
The third day try using the vegetable and fruit diet.
The fourth day use the milk and banana diet.
The fifth day you might use the meat only diet.
The sixth day you can use the meat and vegetable diet.
The seventh day use brown rice and vegetables.

Another interesting variation to our Oriental 7-day diet is based on milk and milk products. You can use this for a one week variation and you can be sure that you will continue to lose pounds, while at the same time satisfying your taste buds.

On any given day you can use yogurt, fruit flavored to give variety. You can use cottage cheese or pot cheese for lunch, with a piece of fruit, such as a pear or peach. For dinner you can eat a cheese omelet, made with two eggs, and fried without fat.

During each day you can drink as many as 6 glasses of skimmed milk, starting at breakfast, and fortify the skimmed milk with powdered milk. This gives added proteins and more energy.

You may drink buttermilk one day, to add variety. You can also vary this diet by eating other cheese products, such as Cheddar or other cheese. Cheese should be used carefully however, as it is a high-calorie food and only a two inch square should be consumed in a day while on this cheese and milk diet plan.

BROWN RICE AND EGG REDUCING PLAN

I have seen many people lose weight quickly on a brown rice and egg diet for one week, which they used to add variety to the above plans.

You can poach or fry an egg and serve it on top of the rice, with a little melted margarine, and this can be eaten as often as three or four times a day. Breakfast can include 8 oz. of orange juice or other fruit juice, one slice of whole-wheat toast, and the egg and rice combination.

You can also vary this egg diet for the week by having, every other day, an egg omelet—one time use cheese for filler, the next time use mushrooms, another time use chips of bacon (out of which all the fat has been removed by frying). Green peppers and onions can be added for another meal. With the omelets you can serve a small portion of rice.

— 13 —

How to Use
the Oriental Diet Plan
to Give You Added Joy
in Love and Sex

In our Oriental 7-day quick weight loss diet, you will experience benefits that go way beyond losing weight safely and pleasantly. You will find that it gives added joy in love and helps prolong the satisfaction that comes in sexual relations beyond the normal span of 60 and 70 years of age.

A healthy, normal interest in love and sex helps give a person a reason for living. A body that is sluggish, fat and chronically exhausted cannot feel the stirrings of fine emotions that a slender person who is in excellent physical condition feels.

I once knew Queen Nazli, the Egyptian mother of King Farouk. She told me of the early years when Farouk ascended the throne in Egypt—he was a slender, handsome young man, with high ideals and a great dream for his undeveloped country. Then, when the young king became surrounded by sycophants, who lured him into every known kind of physical debauchery, including excessive foods and sexual promiscuity, the young king began to deteriorate, until he finally wound up weighing nearly 300 pounds. He became sluggish, his character changed, he lost his dream of achievement for his nation, and was soon forced to abdicate. He lived in exile for the remainder of his life and spent his days in trying to recapture some semblance of his former glory.

The nature of the foods we eat communicates itself to our character formation as well as to the building of the body cells. If you want to add new zest and buoyancy to life, you need to operate on all planes of consciousness. There must be physical well-being, freedom from sickness, plenty of vitality to pursue your goals, sexual and romantic fulfillment, and the soul's higher aspirations for the better, more spiritual life.

THE ORIENTAL DIET PLAN ADDS TO LIFE'S JOYS

One reason why the Oriental diet plan can improve your sexual vigor and give you a more romantic outlook on life is the fact that you will be taking more vitalized, live foods into your body than you were formerly. You will also be able to eat more frequently, at least six times a day, of the vitalizing and yet reducing foods, so that your body receives a constant flow of energy without making you feel sluggish, nervous and exhausted.

A study was made at a famous Eastern university on physical efficiency and sexual vitality. A startling fact was discovered: When a person ate only three regular meals a day, he stuffed his system with many unnecessary foods that lacked nutritive value and affected his energy and his sexual potency. When the meals were reduced in size and the person ate six times a day, it was discovered that he gained in vitality, felt less nervous and irritable and had stronger sexual drives.

What is the reason for this difference? As the body requires certain amino acids, found mostly in protein foods, to function properly, it was found that in three meals a day there was less chance that all of the 22 different amino acids would be taken into the body. But if the meals are increased to six a day, as we suggest in our Oriental system of dieting, there is a good chance that most of these amino acids will be ingested during the six meals per day.

The foods that are richest in these essential elements are meat, fish, cheese, soy beans, and rice in its unprocessed, natural state, where the proteins are left in the husks.

In our balanced reducing diet, and also in the sustaining diet after losing your necessary pounds, you will continue to receive these highly important amino acids that give you feelings of well-being, and which increase sexual vigor and potency.

To show you how this natural food plan works to give one sexual vigor until an advanced age, I cite the case of the noted physical culture expert, Bernarr MacFadden. I met this famous man when he was married to one of my students in Carnegie Hall. Her name was Jonnie Lee, and when she became Mrs. MacFadden, she had a chance to study the health and diet secrets of this man who retained his sexual vigor and zest for life into his late eighties.

In fact, when he was past 80, to prove that he was still as daring as a man of 30, he jumped from a plane with a parachute!

Jonnie told me that Bernarr MacFadden was predominantly a vegetarian, eating little meat, but he was a great believer in live, vitalic foods—eating natural grains, nuts, soy beans, rice in its natural state, vegetables and fruits in season.

MacFadden also believed in fasting and every month for two days he ate no solid foods, living entirely on fruit and vegetable juices. He believed that this flushed the body of lactic acid salts and poisons that had been accumulated from stress and overeating.

MacFadden never ate a full meal three times a day; instead, he nibbled all day long on various proteins, such as nuts, sunflower seeds, pumpkin seeds and sesame seeds. He believed that these live seeds contained valuable lecithin that heightened sexual vigor and potency. He was sexually active until the day he died, in his late eighties!

Perhaps this is a clue as to why our Oriental food plan helps, not only while reducing, but all your life, while you maintain the basic plan with its variations on the sustaining diet to keep you vital and sexually active until an advanced old age.

FOODS THAT ADD TO SEXUAL
POTENCY AND VITALITY

The following foods are high in amino acids and in lecithin, the food supplement that helps in reducing the cholesterol level in the bloodstream. As lecithin has been found to play a vital role in the life function of the living cells, it is thought to be an essential element in maintaining the body's sexual vigor at a high level into advanced old age.

Amino acids are found plentifully in the following foods:

Lean beef, lamb, pork and veal
Soy beans, soy bean oil, soy bean flour, soy bean powder
Fish
Cheese
Beans—navy and lima, as well as lentils (also have some proteins)

Brown rice has some of these essential proteins and amino acids. This is one reason why it is a valuable basic food in any diet, to be eaten at least three or four times a week when on the sustaining diet.

Lecithin is found plentifully in the following foods: soy bean powder and oil (which can be added to cereals for breakfast, or in salads or soups). Lecithin is prominent in certain seeds that can be munched between meals. These include sunflower, pumpkin, and sesame seeds. In fact, these seeds contain even more lecithin than soy beans! They should be eaten daily if one wants sexual vigor and a high degree of vitality and energy.

Mr. T.L. was a man of 60 when I first met him through my lecture work in New York city. He was 30 pounds overweight, weighing 195 pounds, when he should have weighed 165 pounds for his age and height. But being overweight was not his only problem. In our first interview he told me he had been sexually impotent for three years, and his wife had accepted the fact that this was probably due to the aging process. She was five years younger than he was, and still had sexual desires, which she now had to suppress.

Before he began the Oriental system of reducing, I had him

check carefully with his doctor, who gave him the go-ahead signal, as he was in fairly good condition physically. He had slight symptoms of high blood pressure, which varied from time to time. He was a heavy smoker, and drank coffee all day long to keep up his energy for his work.

T.L. responded to the Oriental diet beautifully, and the first week he was able to lose 12 pounds. This encouraged him so that he kept at the diet, with variations, until, in two months' time, he had completely shed the 30 unwanted pounds!

But changing his dietary habits was also necessary if he was to overcome his problem of sexual impotence.

I remembered a Guru I had once met in India who was more than a hundred years of age, and he told me about the wonders of soy bean oil, which is high in lecithin. He also told me about sunflower and pumpkin seeds which he munched on all day between meals. He claimed that these foods contained natural elements that would prolong sexual vigor into the eighties.

I told T.L. about soy bean oil, and also about the sunflower and pumpkin seeds, suggesting that he might try them to increase his sexual potency.

I did not hear anything further from T.L. for about a month, and I had completely forgotten him when one day my telephone rang, and a vigorous, joyous voice on the other end proclaimed, "Well, doc, your soy bean oil and seeds worked miracles! For the first time in several years I am like a young man of thirty! My wife and I are going on our second honeymoon. We're like a couple of kids in love for the first time!"

Since that time I have seen amazing results from the therapy of soy bean oil, soy bean flour, and soy bean powder, as well as from the eating of sunflower, pumpkin and sesame seeds, all of which are rich in lecithin. This should be something that is added to all normal diets, not just on the reducing diet, since it gives the body many important amino acids and other elements that are essential to the maintenance of good health.

Whole-wheat germ, as well as the natural, unprocessed barley, oats, and buckwheat contain vital elements that also give vitality and energy when used in their natural state.

THE IMPORTANCE OF YOUR THYROID GLAND

One of the most important glands that determines how young you remain, and how you retain or lose your sexual vigor, is the thyroid gland that is located in the throat. This gland affects the metabolic rate of the body—if it is too active in its secretion of thyroxin, you will be in a state of constant nervous activity, you will be restless, and you will suffer from insomnia and other symptoms; if it secretes too slowly, then you will find you seldom have enough energy to keep you going through the day and you may drink cups of coffee or smoke dozens of cigarettes to give you the energy boost you feel you need.

One of the vital elements that will keep your body in good health and give you youthful sexual vigor throughout life is iodine. In fact, the thyroid requires iodine to keep it functioning perfectly. It is true that only small amounts of iodine are needed, and these should be from natural foods. (The iodine used for medication on wounds is NOT the type to be used in the diet.) Iodine is found plentifully in fish and also in garlic. Iodized salt is also a good source for obtaining the small amounts one needs, if one eats salt. Some people eat sea salt, which is sold in health food stores and this is also a good source of this vital element. There is also a form of dried kelp or seaweed that can be used for obtaining iodine in the diet.

When the thyroid gland malfunctions it has very serious repercussions in the health, and it affects the sex glands especially. They become sluggish and sometimes inactive, making a person unable to respond to sexual stimulus. When adequate amounts of iron are combined with iodine in the diet, it has tremendous power to implement the sex drive and affects the heart, brain, endocrine system and blood vessels, giving an impetus to all these and making a person sexually vigorous and healthy for old age.

SEX POWER DEPENDS ON
THE MINERALS IN THE DIET

Even when you are on the Oriental reducing diet, keep in

mind that your body must continue to be supplied with minerals and other elements necessary to good nourishment and to keep the body functioning at high levels of energy.

Iron in the blood not only gives that extra boost to sex energy and general vitality, but it is essential to keep the nails, hair, muscles, bones and teeth in good condition. Also, iron is helpful in maintaining the balance between the body's alkalinity and acidity, which can affect the body's chemistry. When there are insufficient minerals in the diet, the health suffers, for iron affects the nerves that send messages to the entire body for its proper functioning. Iron also helps the body assimilate many nutrients that it requires for maintaining perfect health and sexual vigor.

Elsewhere we have discussed the minerals that can be taken in supplements to a diet, if you do not obtain them through natural foods. These necessary minerals are:

Iron
Phosphorus
Calcium
Copper
Manganese
Potassium
Sodium

Iron

Iron is found in its natural state in all green leafy vegetables; also in soybeans, wheat germ, egg yolk, liver, and bran. Blackstrap molasses is also a good source of iron.

Phosphorus

Phosphorus can be obtained in its natural state in most protein foods, such as fish, meats, cheese, poultry, eggs, whole-wheat products and soybeans.

If you do not want to take these minerals in supplements you can take them in foods, but it is easier to be sure you obtain the right amounts by taking one or two vitamin supplements a day; or, consult your doctor as to your exact needs if you have a special condition that needs treatment.

Calcium

If you are getting plenty of calcium in your daily diet but eat a great deal of white bread, chocolates, or absorb the chemical DDT from unwashed vegetables or fruits, you may be killing the absorption of this vital element. Calcium is to be found most plentifully in milk, egg yolk, olives, most cheese products, blackstrap molasses, green vegetables, seafood, poultry, and whole grains.

Copper

When there is a deficiency in this vital mineral a person is apt to have anemia, for copper and iron work together to help enrich the blood. Also, copper plays a part in pigment formation and a lack of it can often cause gray hair prematurely.

Copper is to be found in oatmeal, leafy greens, liver, soybeans, wheat germ, blackstrap molasses, bran and egg yolk. Huckleberries are also rich in this mineral.

Manganese

It is claimed that an absence of this mineral in the daily diet can lead to a lessening of interest in sexual expression. It often has been found to interfere with normal functioning of the reproductive glands. As manganese works with calcium and phosphorus, it helps activate a number of the body's enzymes. You find little of this vital mineral in the refined foods, but it is to be found in cereals, green vegetables, and whole grains. Wheat germ sprinkled over salads or used in breakfast cereals is a good source of this mineral.

Potassium

Potassium is often cooked out of vegetables when they are overcooked. It is best to steam vegetables until you can pass a fork through them and not cook them until they fall apart.

This vital mineral helps the nerves, the heart and muscles, and gives tone and nourishment. When it is lacking in the diet a person may feel irritable, suffer from indigestion and often is constipated.

Those who suffer from insomnia often lack potassium in their diets.

Potassium is to be found in green leafy vegetables, sea kelp, cranberries, tomatoes, apple cider vinegar, blackstrap molasses, cucumbers, carrots and honey. Many fruits also contain this vital mineral.

Sodium

This important mineral is often thought to exist in salt, but it does not, for salt is sodium chloride and does not supply the necessary sodium to the diet. It can be obtained from green string beans, celery, zucchini, and many other vegetables.

In using the Oriental system of dieting, and the sustaining diet after losing weight, keep in mind always, that if you want your body to maintain its youthful vigor and sexual potency until old age, you cannot be 20 to 30 pounds overweight. There is a marked drop in energy when you carry fat around, and it naturally affects your joy in living, as well as your sexual expression and feelings.

I remember once I carried a 20 pound turkey home from the market one holiday. Although it was only two blocks to my house, when I got there I felt exhausted! I thought then that if a person carrying 20 pounds of excess fat 24 hours a day felt the same way, no wonder he could not perform his life's functions and his work efficiently and with joy. Fat robs us of the joy of living, not only in reduced sexual desires but in every other department of our lives.

When you get the weight off with the Oriental reducing system, you can keep it off by following the sensible rules given in this chapter.

— 14 —

How to Satisfy
Your Sweet Tooth on the
Oriental Reducing Diet
Without Adding Weight

While you are on our Oriental diet for losing weight without hunger, you can still eat many wonderful desserts and be safely within your caloric requirements for the day, without the fear of adding weight.

How do the Orientals satisfy their cravings for sweets? They cannot afford the rich starches, sugars and carbohydrates that we eat in this country, and, fortunately for them, they are forced to rely on the natural fruits, dates, figs, honey, and other products that are indigenous to their countries.

ELVIS PRESLEY HAD A WEIGHT PROBLEM ONCE

One summer when I went to Greece to live, I leased my home

for a year to the famous rock and roll star, Elvis Presley. I had occasion to get to know him and I found that he was battling weight even then, early in his career.

We had a poolside lunch one day in June, and he had several guests. The waiters served up generous portions of barbecued frankfurters, hamburgers, and oven baked beans, Southern style. That meant they had plenty of pork and molasses in them. With this they served corn bread dripping with melted butter. The luncheon was lacking in any kind of salads or fruits.

When we were talking about foods and weight, I remarked to Elvis, "If this is the kind of food you eat daily, you will always have a weight problem."

Then I outlined a diet similar to our Oriental reducing diet, which would include energy foods, as well as nutritionally sensible foods that would bring balance into his diet.

When I returned that fall from my trip to Europe and saw Elvis again, I was astounded at how he looked! He had lost 15 pounds and now he was on a sane, balanced diet that included vegetables, some meats, plenty of fruits, and no more sugars, starches and heavy carbohydrate desserts. I have watched Elvis over the years on TV and in movies, and have noticed that he seldom gains or loses weight, and I know that he is probably still following those diet pointers I gave him back at the beginning of his great career.

FRESH FRUIT DESSERTS

Following is a list of the fresh fruits, which may be used in season, for preparing some of the desserts that will give your sweet tooth satisfaction without adding extra weight.

Apples	Mangoes
Apricots	Nectarines
Bananas	Oranges
Blueberries	Papaya
Blackberries	Peaches
Cantaloupe	Pears
Cherries	Persimmons
Currants	Pineapple (fresh or canned)
Gooseberries	Plums

Grapefruit	Raspberries
Grapes	Rhubarb
Guavas	Strawberries
Honeydew melon	Tangerines
Loganberries	Watermelon

Remember, while on the Oriental 7-day diet to lose weight, you do not need to deny your craving for sweets. But it is important to know that you can add the following desserts to your regular diet only by eating smaller portions than if you were not dieting. Any food, if excessively eaten, even meat, adds many unnecessary calories and is converted into fat. This is why later, I shall give you calorie counting as an adjunct to your sustaining diet, so that you will become accustomed to thinking in terms of your required calories and not go overboard on any of the foods you eat in the future.

For some of the exotic desserts given below, you can use a pie crust made the health food way, with whole-wheat flour, and by blending the following ingredients. This will keep in your freezer indefinitely and it may be used as a base for many desserts made with fresh or canned fruits. You will need:

2 cups of whole-wheat flour
1 cup of sour cream
1 teaspoonful of brown sugar
1 cake of yeast
1/4 pound of margarine (if on sustaining diet, use butter)

Blend the brown sugar and the yeast with the sour cream until it is a thick paste, and then let the mixture rise for about an hour.

Use sea salt rather than regular salt and mix this with the margarine or butter. Add the sour-cream mixture, and knead in a bowl. Add more flour if you find the dough sticks in the pan or seems to be too soft, until it is easy to handle. Now roll the dough into a thin pie crust and line bottom of pie plate when you want to add the various fruits we shall give for desserts.

HIMALAYA APRICOT TARTS

Cut in halves a pound of fresh, ripe apricots, place these on the crust just described, and cut into smaller portions in individual small tin dishes. Or, if you choose to make an entire pie, use a pie tin and spread the dough over it, putting in the filler of fruits and other ingredients.

Top the apricots with yogurt which is blended with a tablespoon of honey.

Put into the oven and bake for 30 minutes at about 340 degree heat.

TIBETAN SNOWMAN DESSERT

Use lemon or orange sherbet, or if you choose, raspberry sherbet. Sprinkle cocoanut (shredded) on top, and before serving add a spoonful of grenadine or real rum.

This is a dessert that is low in calories and yet gives the impression of being a real sweet dessert.

PAPAYA SHANGRI-LA

This delicious fruit has many vitamins and minerals that are excellent for any diet, reducing or sustaining. You can cut a papaya in half and stuff the halves with chopped prunes, nuts and a little honey, topped with yogurt. It is rich and flavorful and satisfies the appetite after a light meal, or it may be eaten as a salad at lunch with a slice of date-nut bread.

BOMBAY BANANA BOUQUET

2 sliced bananas
2 tsp. lemon juice
2 egg whites, unbeaten
1 spoonful honey
1 tsp. vanilla
top with nutmeg or cinnamon

Thoroughly mix the banana and the lemon juice by mashing them together, then add the egg white, a touch of sea salt, and the spoonful of honey and vanilla. Blend these all together in your electric blender until they are thoroughly mixed.

Put into four sherbet glasses and top with a touch of cinnamon or nutmeg.

This adds a festive touch to your lunch or dinner, and if you have guests they will think it is a rich dessert, and they will not even know that you are on a diet. The bananas are carbohydrate, of course, but you need some carbohydrates each day, so let this dessert furnish it for this day.

SULTAN'S HAREM AMBROSIA

This dessert may be served in sherbet glasses, either hot or cold. It is slightly stimulating to the emotions as part of the ingredients consists of dry red wine. It is good after a light dinner and gives the impression of being a rich dessert, and yet it has few calories. You need:

4 tablespoons of honey
4 egg yolks
4 tablespoons of red wine

Beat these together until thoroughly blended, and then put them into a pan and apply medium heat until the mixture begins to boil, then turn off heat. Be sure to keep beating the mixture constantly while cooking, until it is thickened and quite fluffy. Put into sherbet dishes and cool, or serve hot.

CLEOPATRA'S SLIMMING NECTAR

To satisfy your taste buds during your 7-day Oriental reducing diet, you can take this delicious fruit drink two or three times a day, between your normal six meals. It will give you valuable minerals and other elements, without adding weight.

Mix together equal parts of cranberry juice, pineapple juice, apricot juice and add the juice of half a lemon. Serve after cooling in the refrigerator.

CASHMERE HONEY PEARS

For this dessert you can use canned pears if fresh pears are not available. Be sure to wash off the syrup or use pears that are dietetically canned, with a sugar substitute. Drain off the juice. Then gather the following:

8 pear halves
1 tbs. honey
1 tbs. lemon juice
1 tsp. cinnamon
2 tbs. margarine

Place the pear halves in a buttered dish, pour the lemon juice and honey over the pears, and sprinkle with cinnamon, with small pieces of margarine on top. Bake in oven heated to 350 degrees for about 15 minutes or less, and serve with cold sour cream on top.

BAGHDAD CUSTARD RICE PUDDING

1/2 cup of brown rice	4 cups milk
1/4 cup brown sugar	4 tbs. water
2 tbs. plain gelatin	1 tsp. vanilla
1 tsp. almond extract	1 cup whipped cream (artificial)

Cook the rice in a double boiler until it is tender, which is usually in about an hour. Be sure to stir it occasionally to keep it from sticking to the pan. Then add the brown sugar and the gelatin. Before adding gelatin and sugar, soak these in cold water about four minutes. Let this stand until cold, and then stir in the vanilla and almond extracts. Put in the refrigerator to chill until ready to serve, then top it with the artificial whipped cream.

BANANAS A LA NIRVANA

Bananas are an excellent source of carbohydrates and should be used frequently in desserts.

This celestial delight is easy to make and very delicious. You will need:

6 or 7 bananas
3 tbs. brown sugar or honey
1/2 tsp. cinnamon
1 tsp. ground ginger
3 tbs. margarine or butter
1/2 lb. creamed cheese
1 cup plain yogurt

Brown the halved bananas slightly in margarine. Then put 6

halves into a slightly buttered pie plate. Mix the brown sugar or honey with the cream cheese and the cinnamon, and spread half of the mixture over the 6 banana halves. Then put the remaining bananas on top and spread the balance of the mixture. Top with the yogurt and place in oven for only 20 minutes at about 350 degrees. This should serve 6.

KASHMIR APRICOT DELIGHT

The apricot is a very valuable food and many people of the Mid East and Far East use them as a dietary staple, either fresh or dried. You can use the dried apricots for this delicious dessert, soaking them in cold water overnight until soft. You will need:

8 to 10 whole apricots
6 egg whites, beaten until stiff
1/4 tsp. artificial salt
5 tbs. honey or brown sugar
1/4 tsp. almond extract

Shred the apricots in a beater until they are pulp. Be sure the eggs are beaten until firm, then put the apricots into the beaten eggs with all the other ingredients. Put into a greased double boiler and cook for an hour.

You can serve this apricot delight with pineapple or grape juice as a sauce. Or you can top it with artificial whipped cream, or a spoonful of sour cream or yogurt.

INDIAN PRINCESS ORANGE TEMPTATION

A simple and yet nutritious and healthy dessert is made with just oranges and shredded cocoanut, and yet it gives an exotic look to your after dinner dessert if you have guests. All you need are

5 oranges (sliced thin)
2/3 cup of shredded cocoanut

On top of a layer of sliced oranges, sprinkle cocoanut, then continue the process, with a layer of oranges, again topped with the shredded cocoanut. Sprinkle chopped nuts on top and chill.

There is a wide variety of fruit cups that you can use for desserts, which add to your meals and give the impression you are having something sweet at the end of your meal, and yet the calories contained in these various fruit cups are few.

You can combine pears and apricots, using canned pears, and canned apricots. Combine these in a compote dish and chill before serving.

Take a can of grapefruit sections and combine these with canned peach halves. Serve them in a glass sherbet dish.

Use a combination of apples, grapefruit slices, and orange slices. Mix these together in a glass sherbet dish and chill before serving.

Use a can of black bing cherries, and a can of purple plums. Mix them together, chill and serve.

A combination of the various types of melons also makes an appetizing and appealing dessert. Use equal balls of honeydew, watermelon and cantaloupe, mixing them together. If you wish to add a special touch put a little grenadine on each dish you serve.

A good combination is also made with cantaloupe and bing cherries combined; also with purple plums and cantaloupe.

Honeydew melon combined with diced oranges is also a good combination.

PHAROAH'S PYRAMID EXOTICA

This interesting sweetmeat can be used as an in-between nibbler to keep you from getting too hungry. You combine dates, figs, honey, almonds (chopped), and shredded cocoanut.

Put the ingredients into a bowl and mix thoroughly. Use about 1 doz. figs, 1 doz. dates, a tablespoon of honey, and about 8 chopped almonds or other nuts. Then mix the shredded cocoanut with the above ingredients, and shape into pyramids, if you wish to serve them to guests, and put them into your refrigerator until ready to serve as an after dinner dessert, or you may keep them indefinitely and nibble on them to kill your appetite.

BOMBAY BLISS

When serving the previous desserts to guests at lunch or dinner, you can add a touch of the romantic or exotic to your meal by giving these desserts interesting names. The Bombay Bliss is an excellent light dessert, made of fruits, but it looks like a heavy calorie dish, which it is NOT. The ingredients needed are:

4 ripe bananas
6 peach halves
6 pear halves
1 cup of raisins (soaked until soft)
3 cups of canned blackberries or raspberries
1/4 cup shredded cocoanut

Line a pie tin with a layer of crumbled graham crackers. Put a layer of sliced bananas, a layer of pears, and a layer of peaches over the crackers. Top with blackberries or raspberries, and add raisins. Then sprinkle with cocoanut, and add a bit of shredded ginger.

To add variety to the above Bombay Bliss you can top the fruit layers with artificial whipped cream, or a cupful of yogurt, or sour cream.

SHANGHAI APPLE WHIP

2 cups of applesauce
5 egg whites beaten until thick
1 tbs. lemon juice
1 tbs. pineapple juice
1/2 tsp. ground ginger
1 tbs. honey or brown sugar

Beat the egg white with the honey added, and then put in the applesauce. Add lemon juice and pineapple juice to the mixture, and pour into glasses to chill before serving. Put a touch of ground ginger on top as garnishing.

ISTANBUL YOGURT—STRAWBERRY DELIGHT

This healthy and tasty dessert adds few calories to your reducing diet and yet gives great satisfaction to the taste buds. It is also attractive to serve to your guests, who will think it exotic and not connect it with dieting at all. You need the following ingredients:

3 cups of strawberries (fresh if possible, if not, frozen will do as well)
2/3 cup yogurt
1/2 tsp. vanilla extract
1/2 tsp. almond extract
4 tsp. honey or artificial sweetener

Mix the yogurt with the washed strawberries, add the vanilla and almond extracts and honey, and mix thoroughly in a bowl. Chill in the refrigerator for an hour or so and serve in glass dishes.

CREME DE MENTHE
BABYLONIAN PINEAPPLE DELIGHT

2 tsp. of grated cocoanut
several slices of pineapple, canned or fresh
3 tbs. of creme de menthe
3 tsp. grated ginger

Use chunks or slices of pineapple; place pineapple in a dessert dish, sprinkle creme de menthe over it, and put grated cocoanut and ginger on top. Garnish with fresh mint leaves, if available. Serve cold.

TAJ MAHAL FRUIT LOVE CUP

A combination of fruits can be used as a tasty variation to your desserts while dieting or even when on your sustaining diet. The Taj Mahal fruit love cup uses the following fruits:

3 cups of cantaloupe or honeydew melon balls, or mixed with watermelon balls
3 oranges cut up into pieces
3 sliced bananas
1 tbs. honey
1 tsp. lemon juice
1/3 cup grated cocoanut

Mix the cantaloupe balls, oranges, and bananas with the honey and lemon juice. Then top with grated cocoanut and chill before serving. To add an exotic touch put a little grenadine on top of each dish.

MAHARAJAH CANTALOUPE A LA ROYALE

This delicious combination of bananas and cantaloupe is an excellent dessert after a meat or fish dinner.

2 bananas
6 tbs. sour cream
2 tsp. honey
1 large cantaloupe

Cut the cantaloupe into one inch cubes, after peeling. Mash the 2 bananas in a bowl and add honey and sour cream, mixing them carefully until thoroughly blended. Now put the pieces of cantaloupe into the mixture and toss. Be sure that the sour cream covers all the fruit thoroughly before serving.

ORIENTAL FRUIT MEDLEY

Use fresh peaches and apricots and plums for this delicious fruit dessert, if in season. However, you can use canned or frozen fruits if you choose. The following are needed:

4 peaches
4 apricots
4 plums
1 tbs. honey
3 ripe or canned plums
3 tsp. lime or lemon juice
3 tsp. pineapple juice

Peel the peaches and apricots when used fresh, and slice them. Mix the honey and lime juice and pineapple juice together and pour over the fruit.

You can add variety to the above by topping with lemon, orange, pineapple or raspberry sherbet.

These desserts, being principally fruit, can be used even while you are on the 7-day Oriental reducing diet without endangering your caloric intake. However, they should be used sparingly, until you have lost your desired pounds. On your sustaining diet they can be used for the rest of your life and they will satisfy your craving for sweets without giving you the additional calories that would soon put your weight back on again.

— 15 —

Count Your Daily Calories for a Lifetime Stay-Slender Food Plan

What should you know about calories? Is it necessary to count calories the rest of your life?

There has been a great deal of controversy over this question for many years. Calorie counters say that if one eats food that contains more calories than the body needs for its daily energy requirements it will be turned into fat.

There is truth to this statement, for the body can only absorb a certain amount of caloric energy per day. If the body is overloaded with calories it has only one recourse: to convert the unnecessary calories into body fat. Then the fat has to be taken off or there are serious health conditions, as well as unsightly physical conditions to bear.

The consequences of NOT counting calories can readily be seen in the statistics that come out each day on what happens to obese people who have let their calories run away with them. A recent example was that of a famous female singer who weighed 276 pounds and was found dead in her hotel room from a heart condition due to her obesity. Upon performing an autopsy, the physicians found that her heart muscles had begun to turn to fat, impeding their function and leading to a fatal heart attack.

While you are on our Oriental 7-day diet for quick weight loss, it is not necessary to count your calories. The reason for this, as stated earlier, is that you can hardly overeat the reducing vegetables given in the food plan, and that you can hardly take more rice than the body requires for each day's activity. Rice is very filling and a little goes a long way. Then when you add meat to the Oriental system of losing weight without hunger, you eat only a small portion each day, and if it is lean meat, this can hardly add enough calories to become a serious problem.

As carbohydrates are practically eliminated in the Oriental diet plan, except for those found in vegetables, there is little concern about starches, sugars and fats. But when you go on the sustaining diet and eat a balanced meal, including fats, starches, sugars, and proteins, it is obvious that you could soon return to your former state of obesity if you do not restrict your food intake and avoid the high calories that most people take in each meal. The following figures will reveal how few calories the average person needs to remain healthy and slender.

Sex	Height	Weight	Age	Calories per day
MALE	5'10"	150	20-29	1750
			30-29	1750
			40-49	1700
			50-59	1650
			60-69	1600
			70-79	1550
FEMALE	5'2"	125	20-29	1380
			30-39	1360
			40-49	1340
			50-59	1300
			60-69	1260
			70-79	1230

You will notice that the caloric requirements lessen with age. Also, the above caloric requirements are for people who lead a fairly sedentary life, where there is little exercise or physical labor.

If there is a great deal of physical labor and muscle movement then the calorie requirements rise, but a person who is so active seldom puts on weight, no matter how much he eats.

It is the person who has little exercise and no hard work that can get along on the minimum calorie requirements given above.

Children from the age of 14 to young people of 18 or more, require slightly more calories, as their activities generally eat up the fat before it is put onto their bodies.

Most overweight problems, it is true, are caused because a person takes more calories into his body than he requires for his daily activities. The body has no other recourse but to store these unwanted and unneeded calories as fatty tissue.

To show you how serious is this problem of obesity, last year alone the American public spent more than $400,000,000 on reducing pills, health spas for losing weight, and other methods of weight reduction. Most of these methods achieve the objective of removing unwanted fat, but when the person goes back on his so-called normal diet, he puts the unwanted pounds back again, and the whole vicious cycle has to be repeated again and again.

WHAT YOU SHOULD KNOW ABOUT CALORIES

A calorie is a unit of heat, and has been defined by scientists as the amount of heat required to raise about 2 pounds of water just one degree centigrade. When you ingest food, calories are supplied that the body requires to combine with oxygen, so it can distribute this digested food to all the body tissues.

To get an idea of the caloric energy released by various foods consider the following: 1 teaspoon of white sugar provides 16 calories; 1 teaspoon of olive oil, which is pure fat, releases 36 calories.

Fat produces more calories than protein or carbohydrates. That is one reason why the Oriental reducing plan helps lose weight quickly, because there is little or no fat content to the foods eaten.

A good way to determine your normal caloric requirements for each day is to find your most desirable weight for your height and age, and then choose the number of calories that fit your requirements.

If you are a sedentary worker, that is, you do not have much physical activity each day, you can determine your required daily calories by multiplying the figure 10 by your normal weight. If you are a man and weigh 175 pounds, and are a sedentary worker, your average caloric requirements per day would be about 1,750 calories.

If you are a woman and weigh 125 pounds your ideal caloric intake per day would be 1,250 calories. The moment you absorb more calories in your daily food intake than that, it begins to be stored as excess fat.

However, if you are fairly active in your daily work, and move around a good deal, or exercise moderately, such as walking, swimming or playing golf or tennis, then your caloric requirements would be changed. You would multiply your ideal weight by the figure 15, and obtain the amount of calories you need per day.

For a 175 pound man who is fairly active, the caloric intake would now be raised to about 2,625 calories per day.

For a woman of 125 pounds, who is fairly active and does some moderate exercise, the caloric intake would now be changed to about 1875 calories per day.

If you do very heavy manual work that requires a great deal of muscular effort and movement, then you would multiply your ideal weight by the figure 20 to obtain your ideal caloric intake. This would raise the caloric requirements for a man weighing 175 pounds to about 3,500 calories per day.

For a woman weighing 125 pounds, who does very heavy work with great muscular activity, you would multiply 125 by the figure 20, and this would give about 2500 calories per day, as required to maintain the body at normal levels of energy expenditure.

Here are some typical activities showing the caloric energy expended per hour, which will help you understand more about the caloric requirements for your personal needs. The following estimates are for a person weighing about 160 pounds.

Riding a bicycle burns up about 200 calories per hour.

Boxing requires about 780 calories per hour.

Dancing burns up about 260 calories per hour.

Washing dishes requires about 70 calories an hour.

Eating uses up about 26 calories per hour.

Horseback riding, at a trot, requires about 300 calories per hour.

Fencing, being rather strenuous, uses up about 500 calories per hour.

Piano playing requires about 100 calories per hour.

Table tennis requires about 305 calories per hour.

Rowing a boat, in competition with others, burns up 1,120 calories per hour.

Running takes up about 500 calories per hour. This is one reason why jogging has become a popular form of exercise.

Swimming takes about 550 calories per hour.

Typewriting consumes only about 70 calories an hour.

Walking, rapidly, takes 240 calories per hour.

Sweeping floor, with vacuum cleaner, requires about 200 calories per hour.

It can be seen that the more strenuous forms of exercise tend to burn up calories more quickly than the milder forms of exercise. Very often, when the caloric intake is high, you can burn up those fat-producing extra calories by indulging in some form of exercise that will help melt the fat away.

However, the best thing is to know your calories and figure out how many you need per day, then automatically cut your food intake to those required calories.

Jessie R. was a typical housewife with the usual housework that required about 300 calories an hour for the normal activities such as vacuuming the floor, washing dishes, dusting, shopping, and preparing the meals. However, as she did not work at all these tasks a full 8 hours a day (doing her usual housework in about 3 hours), she spent a great deal of time in watching her favorite romantic stories on TV, and as she had no children to take care of, this pastime consumed several hours a day.

While watching TV Jessie often nibbled on chocolates, and at night, she and her husband had little tidbits, which added considerably to her caloric intake.

When I met Jessie R. she had gained 25 pounds in the three years of her marriage and she couldn't understand why. I checked out her dietary habits and found she was serving mashed potatoes with the evening meal, with heavy, starchy gravy; at least two times a week she served spaghetti or macaroni (owing to the high cost of meats); and the desserts were usually something heavy, like pies, ice creams, or fruits canned in heavy syrup.

The caloric intake was way beyond the normal 1,200 to 1,500 per day that Jessie would ordinarily require to do the work she did. She was consuming at least 2,500 calories a day, and all these extra calories were being rapidly turned into fatty deposits on her hips and stomach.

It was necessary for Jessie to cut down on her calories to at least 1,000 per day, for her work output. She was able to get rid of the 25 extra pounds within three weeks on the Oriental diet and then she went on the sustaining diet, allowing herself about 1,500 calories a day for her normal routine. She seemed to hold her weight down to normal in the ensuing months.

When you have once determined the number of calories you require for your particular age and your activities for any given day, you can determine each day's caloric intake and then try to approximate it. If you find yourself putting on a few extra pounds, or you carelessly eat too many carbohydrate and starchy foods, cut down on your fat calories for a few days. Then when you are back to your normal weight, you can resume your normal diet.

It is perfectly natural for you to vary five pounds one way or the other in your monthly weight. Do not be alarmed at these fluctuations, but if you should go over the five pound mark, immediately start your Oriental diet, eating more brown rice and vegetables, and fewer starches and carbohydrates. In one week you will shed the extra pounds without effort.

I have calculated the caloric contents of all the major foods that you may eat in the future and these have been added in the appendix of this book. Consult this list to find out the approximate calories that your general diet contains. Then figure out your menu according to this caloric list so you never go beyond your normal caloric intake for each day.

Very soon you will find yourself so expert in judging your caloric intake that you will automatically form the habit of selecting the right foods for your particular age and weight.

In the following chapter we shall learn some of the Oriental techniques for maintaining a good mental attitude through philosophy and daily meditation. This will help you develop the balance you need to keep you in perfect mental, emotional and physical health.

— 16 —

Add Yoga Power to Your Oriental System of Reducing Without Hunger

Millions of people throughout the world today are using Yoga power to help them achieve mastery of their minds and bodies.

It is vitally important in our Oriental system of reducing without hunger to utilize this regime of control to make it easier for you to keep weight off, as well as to give you the mental power to stay on your reducing diet until you have achieved the desired results.

What does the word Yoga mean? It literally means to be yoked to a higher power than the ordinary conscious mind which we all possess. It admits of a system of mental and physical control that enlists the aid of higher forces within the mind, which psychologists call the subconscious and superconscious minds.

Many Yogis, using mind control alone, have regulated the

metablolism of their bodies so that the body threw off many of the foods that produce fat deposits.

Now in scientific research in what is called alpha biofeedback training, the mind is shown to release brainwaves that are called Alpha, Theta, and Beta. In each of these states of brainwave activity, produced by a high degree of concentration called Meditation, the person trying to control his mind and his body is able to regulate such things as his heart action, his digestion, his blood pressure and other vital functions of the body, including the metabolic processes that determine what foods the body shall absorb and what foods it shall throw off.

By using Yoga meditation during your times of reducing you will avoid the nervousness, fatigue and stress that often come to people who try to reduce or change their food habits in any way. As you will be adopting a new food plan for the rest of your life after losing the desired pounds, it is vitally important that you know how to use Yoga power to avoid the side effects that come from dieting or maintaining the lifetime sustaining diet.

Ella D., a woman who came to me for help in solving her weight problem, weighed 185 pounds. She was very short and her normal weight should have been 120, for her age and height. She had tried various diets to lose weight but found that she could not stay on them for more than a few days at a time. She said, "I get highly tense and nervous when I am dieting. I suppose I use food as an outlet for my emotional frustrations and problems at home."

It was then that she told me the real reason for seeking me out: she and her husband had not been getting along well for several months. As she gained weight he had lost interest in her sexually. She was 46 years of age, and she said her husband no longer found her sexually appealing. She suspected he was seeing another woman, for he was 48 and she knew that he should still be at the peak of his sexual vigor.

I knew that this woman needed more than a weight-losing regime to solve her emotional problems. She needed a life philosophy that would make it easier for her to diet and also to solve her marital problems after she lost her unwanted pounds.

It was very difficult for this woman to remain on the Oriental diet, for she felt a craving for sweets constantly. I gave her one dessert a day that she could indulge in without adding too many extra calories, and then I made her practice the various states of meditation to gain control of her mind and her nerves.

It was amazing to see the change that came over this woman. By the time she had lost her weight, which took her three months of real work, she had become so agreeable and free from tension that her husband began to show romantic interest again, and told her she was like the girl he had married years before. In fact, when she had finally gotten down to her 120 pounds, she had to have a complete new wardrobe, which he gladly bought for her and as an extra bonus, he surprised her by taking her to Hawaii for a second honeymoon!

ORIENTAL REGIMEN FOR KEEPING YOUR WEIGHT DOWN

1. Adopt a philosophy of peace and quiesence in your everyday life. See the events in the outer world as a panorama that is being projected on a giant motion picture screen. View it with interest but not with alarm. Do not let yourself react to the violence, confusion and discord that is in the outer world. View it all as a spectator—do not react with tension, alarm, nervousness and excitability. The Buddha is pictured throughout the Orient as a calm figure, with imperturbable features that reflect only peace and quiet.

The reason this is vitally important in helping you control your body and its metabolism is that when you are quiet and calm within, your body's metabolism is favorably affected. Your heart action will be normal, your blood pressure will remain perfect, and your body will respond with the perfect functioning of all your glands and other organs.

2. Combine, with this exercise to maintain your peace and quiet, the breathing techniques used for achieving tranquility. Oxygen is the perfect tranquilizer. You breathe every moment, because this is one of the most important functions of the body for maintaining life. It is more important than food or water. You can live for days without food, as the body feeds on its own fat when it is deprived of food; you can live for three or four days

without water; but you cannot live more than a few moments without air. This is why the Yogis practice breathing techniques frequently, which help the body burn up the foods that have been ingested and distribute it through the bloodstream to build the body cells.

The breath to practice for achieving this state of calmness is practiced in Hatha Yoga, which is for the maintenance of the body's strength, health and energy. Breathe in to the count of four; hold the breath to the count of four and then breath out to the count of four. Do this five to ten times, at least three times a day, and flush out the fatigue acids, toxins and other chemical wastes that gather in the bloodstream.

This is the tranquilizing breath of Yoga, which helps soothe the nerves and which causes the heart action to be normal, the metabolism to be perfect and the glands to operate normally.

How a Man Used Tranquilizing Breath to Overcome Weight Problem and Bad Temper

It is a well known fact that oxygen intake is nature's way of oxidizing the body and helping the processes of metabolism and absorption of the foods eaten.

When the mind is constantly disturbed and the emotions get out of control, it has a drastic effect on the metabolism as well as on the glandular system.

Robert W. was a 200 pound executive in a large manufacturing plant. He not only had high blood pressure, and symptoms of a serious heart ailment, but his temper flared frequently and he was highly nervous, tense and anxious about the future. All these things contributed to his tendency to overeat and to keep gaining weight.

Robert W. was thoroughly checked by his family doctor, who told him he must lose weight if he wanted to avoid serious health complications. The man came into our lecture work, forced by his wife, who had been a former member, and she got him on the Oriental reducing diet. But with his temper, impatience, and tendency to disbelieve in anything connected with meditation, Yoga, and other forms of philosophy, he simply could not see himself becoming a student of philosophy.

However, when he began to see the fat melting away, under the Oriental system of dieting without hunger, he changed his mind and began to come to regular classes on meditation.

He started the tranquilizing breath with meditation and soon he had lowered his blood pressure to near normal and had such control of his mind that his temper outbursts were completely overcome. He is now on the way to perfect health.

3. When you awaken in the morning adopt your philosophy for the entire day. View the world as being a wonderful place in which to live. Thank God for another day of life and then dedicate your mind, body and soul to your Creator. A good meditation to achieve this oneness with creative life energy is the following:

> I thank God for another day of life. I now dedicate my mind to the reception of inspirational ideas for the betterment of the world. I dedicate my breath as a living prayer to God. Each time I breathe I direct my breath to be a living prayer to the greater glory of God. I dedicate my body as a chalice to the flow of God's life power, so I may be strong and healthy and better serve Him and humanity.

> I direct my body and all its functions to operate at a peak of efficiency, so I shall be strong, healthy and have youthful vitality throughout my natural life span.

I learned of this dedication ceremony from a Tibetan monk I once met in the northern part of India, within view of the Himalayas. He was resting under a tree at noontime, and he was turning a prayer wheel. I stopped to photograph him, and I asked him what he was doing. He then explained that every time his prayer wheel turned, a hundred prayers, attached to the wheel, ascended to the celestial heights. Then he told me how to be in perpetual touch with the cosmic life energy that gives us perfect power for every day's living. By dedicating our mind, body and soul to God each day when we awaken, we are in touch with the source of life and power. The word Yoga literally means to be yoked to the power that created us and which sustains us.

4. Adopt the Oriental attitude that your soul will live forever and that there is no need for the hustle and bustle which catches us up and wears us down. One of the reasons why so many millions of people in this country are sick mentally and physically,

is that they live under pressure. The stresses of modern living, with its daily shocks and tragedies, tends to upset the emotional balance of the average person. This in turn affects the nervous system and the heart, blood pressure, metabolism and other vital functions of the body, including the secretions of the glands. When a person is in a state of perpetual shock, his nervous reactions are such that they release adrenalin into the blood stream. This in turn accelerates the heart and the blood pressure, causing it to become erratic. A chemical is released into the bloodstream, known as epinephrine, which can poison the body and paralyze the body's normal functions. Most people are in a perpetual state of shock from the rapidly shifting, tragic scene of events in the outer world and they react so emotionally that their bodies never recover from these recurring shocks.

Oriental philosophy will help you maintain a state of calm and to adjust to the changing scene with inner poise and equanimity.

5. Repeat the following tranquilizing statements several times a day when you are faced with emotional turmoil.

> My mind is like a peaceful lake without a ripple on the surface. I am peaceful and calm and no outer winds of misfortune can disturb the center of my being where there is only calm and tranquility.

> I ascend to the spiritual mountain top where I rise above the world of war, disaster, sickness and death. On this mountain peak I see into the illimitable vistas of eternity. I rise above my problems into a stratosphere of spiritual poise and power. I look up at the perpetual glory of God's infinite universe and remove myself from the scenes of turbulence and tragedy.

A WOMAN WAS SAVED FROM COMPLETE COLLAPSE BY MEDITATION

Mrs. Sadie J. had been a widow for only three years, but her grief at losing her husband of 30 years was so overwhelming that she lost all desire to live. When I met her she was brought to me by her oldest son, who said they had taken their mother to a psychiatrist to help her overcome her melancholy. The therapy had not helped and they thought my work might assist her in regaining her emotional balance.

Mrs. J. was only ten pounds overweight, and this she was able to lose in one week on the Oriental diet, but I realized that she had to have a sustaining philosophy to keep her alive and to give her a future goal towards which she could aspire.

I showed Mrs. J. how to go into daily meditation, using the Alpha brainwave techniques (what is known as Hatha Yoga in India), and she began to respond from the very first day. I told her to withdraw into her beautiful memories of the happy, romantic 30 years she had spent with her perfect husband and three times daily, to do these meditations. I did not urge her, as some therapists might have, to forget the past and live for the future, for as a student of Mysticism, I realized that the Dream is often more real than reality. By going back over her memory paths of the joyous years with her husband, she was keeping alive the memory and easing the pain of his death. In two months' time she was ready to begin her mental journey into the future. She was soon so strong mentally and emotionally that she could face going out socially once more. Soon she was attending senior dances and having a joyous time. Her son reported to me six months later that his mother had met a retired doctor who had a beautiful home in the country and had asked her to marry him! Whether she does or does not marry, Mrs. J. is on the way to a happy, zestful life because she discovered the secret strength that can come when a person becomes spiritually oriented by a deep, abiding faith and meditation.

MAN IS A THREE-DIMENSIONAL BEING

Man operates on three planes of consciousness: he is mental, physical and spiritual. Only when you learn to operate on these three planes of consciousness do you achieve perfect balance between the mind, body and soul.

In attempting any system of dieting, realize that "Man shall not live by bread alone." It is necessary that you have an adequate spiritual philosophy to sustain you and give you that balance which all great mystics have told us is essential to healthy, happy and successful living.

Now you have the keys that are needed to open the doors of consciousness. The sustaining diet that will keep you healthy and well nourished should be followed all the days of your life.

Do not worry if you do put on a few extra pounds occasionally. Check your weight daily on the bathroom scales, and the moment the weight goes up five or six pounds, go right back on the Oriental quick weight loss diet and you can keep that weight down without effort in the future.

Keep your mind and emotions under control, through the Oriental philosophy we have given in this book, and use meditation and prayer daily to keep your soul attuned to the spiritual power back of the universe.

As you now journey into the future, new and exciting experiences await you! You have learned how to live under the natural laws of the universe, using natural foods that God gave man to sustain him in perfect health. With your good health and normal weight, you will be ready for the greatest adventures of your life, with perfect health and energy to sustain you for a hundred years or more of zestful, joyous living!

Appendix

The following list of foods and their caloric content must be understood to be approximate, for it is difficult to evaluate the exact caloric content of food. However, most nutritional experts come close to agreement on the number of calories in most basic foods.

MEATS

(Calories are estimated for a 4 oz. serving of meat.)

BEEF:

hamburger, broiled and fat removed	210 cal.
boiled beef	235 cal.
filet mignon	200 cal.
broiled liver	165 cal.
pot roast	245 cal.
corned beef	260 cal.
baked beef heart	125 cal.
prime ribs of beef, roasted	190 cal.
sirloin steak	210 cal.
broiled sweetbreads	190 cal.
baked heart	130 cal.

stewed kidneys	190 cal.
tripe (stewed)	118 cal.
beef tongue boiled	310 cal.
round steak broiled	180 cal.
calf brains	145 cal.

CHICKEN:

broiled	150 cal.
boiled	240 cal.
creamed chicken, (1/2 cup)	210 cal.
roast breast chicken	165 cal.
roast leg of chicken	210 cal.

DUCK:

Roast duck	360 cal.

GOOSE:

Roast goose	375 cal.

LAMB:

lamb chops	230 cal.
roast leg of lamb	215 cal.
mutton chops	210 cal.
boiled mutton	205 cal.
roast leg of mutton	355 cal.

PORK:

pork chops (broiled)	220 cal.
baked ham	180 cal.
deviled ham (1 tbs.)	85 cal.
smoked ham	180 cal.
roast loin of pork	210 cal.
fried sausage	400 cal.
bacon (crisp, broiled—4 strips)	120 cal.

SAUSAGE:

bologna	255 cal.
liverwurst	285 cal.
pork (1 normal length)	90 cal.
salami	525 cal.
frankfurters (1 average)	145 cal.

TURKEY:

    breast of turkey roasted   215 cal.

    dark meat   225 cal.

    roast goose   375 cal.

VEAL:

    broiled veal cutlets   180 cal.

    fried cutlets   245 cal.

    roast leg of veal   180 cal.

FISH

Abalone broiled (3 1/2 oz.)	108 cal.
Bass, broiled or baked (4 oz.)	180 cal.
Bluefish, baked or broiled (4 oz.)	180 cal.
Caviar (2 tbs.)	70 cal.

CLAMS:

    canned (3 oz.)   44 cal.

    cherrystone (4 oz.)   90 cal.

    little neck (4 oz.)   90 cal.

    steamed (6—with butter)   140 cal.

COD: (4 oz.)   100 cal.

    codfish balls (small, 2)   75 cal.

    baked codfish (1 medium size)   125 cal.

    dry codfish (1 oz.)   105 cal.

    salted codfish (4 oz.)   140 cal.

    cod steak (1 med. piece)   100 cal.

CRAB:

    cracked crab (1 med. size)   95 cal.

    hard shell (4 oz.)   95 cal.

    soft shell (4 oz.)   90 cal.

FINNAN HADDIE (4 oz.)   100 cal.

    smoked (4 oz.)   100 cal.

Flounder (4 oz.)	75 cal.
Gefilte fish (4 oz.)	75 cal.

HADDOCK (1 fillet)	160 cal.
creamed (4 oz.)	150 cal.
fried	165 cal.
Halibut broiled (4 oz.)	135 cal.
HERRING: (4 oz.)	215 cal.
pickled herring	105 cal.
pickled herring with sour cream	250 cal.
smoked herring	245 cal.
LOBSTER:	
baked or broiled (1 average size)	125 cal.
lobster creamed (4 oz.)	155 cal.
lobster with butter	300 cal.
lobster cocktail (1 average)	80 cal.
1/2 cup meat with sauce	100 cal.
1/2 cup meat with lemon	75 cal.
1/2 cup meat with mayonnaise	95 cal.
lobster Newburgh (1/2 cup)	125 cal.
lobster thermador (1 lobster)	210 cal.
OYSTERS:	
fried (3 large pieces)	250 cal.
raw (4 oz.)	100 cal.
stewed (8 oz. cup)	250 cal.
scalloped (6)	250 cal.
oyster stew—1/2 cream (8 oz. cup)	200 cal.
Porgy (4 oz.)	110 cal.
Red fish (4 oz.)	100 cal.
Red snapper (4 oz.)	95 cal.
SALMON:	
baked or broiled (medium portion)	205 cal.
chinook salmon (4 oz.)	175 cal.
smoked salmon (4 oz.)	285 cal.
SARDINES:	
oil drained off (3 oz.)	180 cal.
with oil (3 oz.)	288 cal.
with tomato sauce (3 oz.)	185 cal.

SCALLOPS:

      broiled (4 oz.)   175 cal.

      fried (4 oz.–3 large pieces)   295 cal.

Seafood au gratin (1/2 cup)   300 cal.

Shad (4 oz.)   190 cal.

Shad Roe (2 oz.)   100 cal.

SHRIMPS:

      canned (3 oz.)   110 cal.

      fresh shrimps (6 med.)   75 cal.

      fried shrimps (6 med.)   100 cal.

      shrimp cocktail (1/3 cup with sauce) 85 cal.

      shrimp creole (6 shrimp w. sauce) 160 cal.

SMELTS:

      fried with butter (2-3)   150 cal.

SOLE:

      fillet of sole (4 oz.)   100 cal.

      sauted (4 oz.)   236 cal.

SQUID:

      dried (4 oz.)   305 cal.

Smoked sturgeon (3 oz.)   110 cal.

Sword fish (1 piece)   223 ca¹

TROUT:

      brook trout (4 oz.)   50 cal.

      smoked (3 oz.)   100 cal

TUNA:

      canned, drained (3 oz.)   175 cal.

      canned, with oil (3 oz.)   245 cal.

      creamed tuna (4 oz.)   270 cal.

      fresh tuna (3 oz.)   150 cal.

      smoked tuna (3 oz.)   130 cal.

      casserole of tuna (1 average portion, with noodles)   300 cal.

VEGETABLES

ARTICHOKES:

canned hearts (5)	37 cal.
Jerusalem (4 small)	78 cal.
bottoms of artichokes (1 normal)	30 cal.

ASPARAGUS:

cooked stalks (6)	22 cal.
cut spears (3/4 cup)	45 cal.
canned (6 spears)	22 cal.
frozen (6 spears)	22 cal.

Bamboo shoots (4 oz.)   30 cal.

BEANS:

baked, with pork, brown sugar or molasses (1 cup)	325 cal.
canned baked beans (1 cup)	325 cal.
tomato sauce (1 cup)	295 cal.
green beans, cooked (1 cup)	27 cal.
green beans, canned (3/4 cup)	50 cal.
kidney beans (7 tbs.)	180 cal.
lima beans (1/2 cup cooked)	180 cal.
lima beans, canned (1 cup)	175 cal.
lima beans, frozen (4 oz.)	130 cal.

Bean Sprouts (1 cup)   27 cal.

BEETS:

beet greens (1/2 cup cooked)	40 cal.
raw beets (2 medium)	105 cal.
cooked beets (1/2 cup)	55 cal.
canned beets (1/2 cup)	60 cal.
pickled beets (1 cup)	55 cal.

BROCCOLI:

cooked (1 cup)	44 cal.
frozen broccoli (2-3 spears)	20 cal.

Brussel Sprouts cooked, (1 cup)   44 cal.

CABBAGE:

    shredded (1 cup)   24 cal.
    Chinese cabbage (1 cup)   15 cal.

CARROTS:

    raw (1)   21 cal.
    raw, grated (1 cup)   45 cal.
    cooked (1 cup)   44 cal.
    canned (1 cup)   44 cal.

CAULIFLOWER:

    buds (1 cup)   25 cal.
    cooked (1 cup)   30 cal.
    frozen (1 cup)   35 cal.

CELERY (1 large stalk)   7 cal.

    cooked (1 cup)   18 cal.

Chard leaves and stalks cooked (1 cup)   30 cal.
Chives chopped (4 oz.)   30 cal.
Chicory (5-6 leaves)   18 cal.
Collards (1 cup)   76 cal.
Coriander (4 oz.)   140 cal.

CORN: (1 ear)   150 cal.

    canned with liquid (1 cup)   170 cal.
    corn fritters (1)   50 cal.

Cucumbers (1 med.)   12 cal.
Dandelion greens (3/4 cup cooked)   75 cal.
Egg Plant (1/2 cup)   52 cal.
Endive (10 leaves)   6 cal.
Escarole (2 large leaves)   6 cal.
Fennel (1 cup)   8 cal.
Garlic (1 clove)   5 cal.
Ginger root (4 oz.)   55 cal.
Hominy grits (1/2 cup cooked)   65 cal.
Horse-radish (1 tbs.)   12 cal.
Kale (1/2 cup cooked)   55 cal.
Kohlrabi, cooked (8 oz.)   72 cal.
Leeks (3 medium)   42 cal.
Lentils (3/4 cup)   315 cal.

Lettuce (1 head)   68 cal.
Lotus root (2/3 segment)   49 cal.

MUSHROOMS:

    fresh, (8 oz.–sliced)   20 cal.
    sauted (7 small)   60 cal.
    canned (1 cup with liquid)   28 cal.

Mustard greens, cooked (1 cup)   30 cal.
Mustard, dry (1 tsp.)   10 cal.
Okra, cooked (1/2 cup)   20 cal.

OLIVES:

    green (10 large)   105 cal.
    ripe or black (10 large)   135 cal.
    stuffed (5 large)   55 cal.

ONIONS:

    raw (1 medium)   49 cal.
    cooked (1 cup)   79 cal.
    green onions (6 small)   23 cal.
    scalloped onions (1/2 cup)   70 cal.
    fried onions (1/2 cup)   162 cal.
    creamed onions (1/2 cup)   109 cal.

PARSNIPS, cooked (1/2 cup)   47 cal.

    raw (4 oz.)   78 cal.

PEAS:

    black-eyed (1 cup)   150 cal.
    fresh cooked, (1 cup)   111 cal.
    canned with liquid (1 cup)   168 cal.
    frozen peas (1/2 cup)   14 cal.
    split peas (1 cup)   14 cal.
    fresh garden peas shelled (4 oz.)   90 cal.

PEPPERS:

    green peppers (1 medium)   16 cal.
        stuffed (1 medium)   185 cal.
    red pepper, dried (1 tbs.)   52 cal.
        fresh (1 med.)   28 cal.
        cooked (1 med.)   17 cal.

PICKLES:

chow chow (4 pcs.)	7 cal.
cucumber pickles (4 slices)	20 cal.
dill pickles (1 med.)	15 cal.
sweet pickles (1 large)	22 cal.
sour pickle (1 large)	15 cal.
sweet mixed relish with mustard (1 tbs.)	16 cal.
sweet mixed relish (1 tbs.)	14 cal.

Pimento (1 medium canned)	10 cal.
Potato chips (10)	108 cal.

POTATOES:

au gratin (4 oz.)	250 cal.
baked or boiled (1 med.)	100 cal.
creamed (3-4 small)	130 cal.
french fried (10 pieces)	157 cal.
hash brown (1 cup)	470 cal.
frozen french fried (10 pieces)	148 cal.
mashed, with milk (1/2 cup)	80 cal.
mashed with butter (1/2 cup)	120 cal.
baked, with peel (1 med.)	102 cal.
baked without peel, med.	97 cal.
boiled, peeled (1 medium)	180 cal.
boiled unpeeled (1 lb.)	359 cal.

Pumpkin (4 oz.)	105 cal.
Radishes (4 small)	7 cal.
Rice, cooked (8 oz. cup)	205 cal.
Sauerkraut (1/4 cup drained)	27 cal.
Scallions (4 med.)	8 cal.
Soy beans (1/2 cup)	120 cal.
Soybean sprouts (1 cup)	60 cal.

SPINACH

cooked (1 cup)	46 cal.
raw (1/2 lb.)	44 cal.
canned (1 cup)	46 cal.

SQUASH:

hubbard or winter baked (1/2 cup)	50 cal.
summer squash boiled (1/2 cup)	20 cal.

String beans (1/2 cup)   25 cal.

SWEET POTATOES:

    baked (1)   140 cal.
    candied (1 small)   314 cal.
    boiled (1 lb.)   560 cal.

TOMATOES:

    canned (8 oz. cup)   46 cal.
    fresh (1 med.)   30 cal.
    stewed (9 oz.)   50 cal.

Turnip tops (1/2 cup)   49 cal.
Turnips cooked (1/2 cup)   22 cal.
Watercress (1 lb.)   180 cal.
Watercress (10 pcs.)   2 cal.

YAMS:

    cooked (1 cup)   260 cal.
    baked (1 cup)   183 cal.
    candied (1 small)   314 cal.

Zucchini (1/2 cup)   23 cal.

FRUITS

APPLE (1 med. raw)   85 cal.

    baked with sugar   200 cal.
    cooked, unsweetened   120 cal.
    dried, cooked and sweetened (1/4 cup)   102 cal.

APPLESAUCE:

    canned, sweetened (8 oz.)   260 cal.
    unsweetened (8 oz.)   120 cal.

APRICOTS:

    canned in syrup, (4 med.)   97 cal.
    dried apricots, cooked unsweetened (1/2 cup)   130 cal.
    stewed (8 oz.)   400 cal.

Avocado (1/2)   280 cal.

BANANAS (1 large)   120 cal.

    fried (1 med.)   140 cal.

BLACKBERRIES, fresh (1 cup)   82 cal.
    canned with syrup (8 oz. cup)   245 cal.
    frozen, sweetened (1 cup)   160 cal.

BOYSENBERRIES:
    frozen, sweetened (1 cup)   160 cal.
    frozen, unsweetened (1 cup)   70 cal.

BLUEBERRIES, fresh (1 cup)   85 cal.
    canned with syrup (8 oz.)   245 cal.
    frozen, sweetened (1 cup)   160 cal.

Cantaloupe (1/2 med. size)   37 cal.
Casaba melon (1 wedge)   52 cal.

CHERRIES, fresh (1 cup)   64 cal.
    canned (8 oz. cup)   94 cal.

Cocoanut (1 med. piece)   161 cal.
    shredded, sweetened (8 oz. cup)   349 cal.

CRANBERRIES (8 oz.)   54 cal.
    cranberry sauce, sweetened (8 oz.)   549 cal.

Dates (3 or 4)   100 cal.

FIGS (2 or 3)   90 cal.
    canned w. syrup (3 figs)   130 cal.
    dried figs (1 large)   57 cal.

Fruit cocktail, canned (6 oz.)   110 cal.
Gooseberries (8 oz.)   60 cal.

GRAPES (4 oz.)   80 cal.
    Thompson seedless (8 oz. cup)   150 cal.

GRAPEFRUIT (1/2 large)   104 cal.
    canned, sweetened (8 oz.)   180 cal.
    canned, unsweetened (8 oz.)   90 cal.

Honeydew melon (1 med. wedge)   49 cal.
Lemon (1 med.)   40 cal.

LOGANBERRIES (2/3 cup)   70 cal.

    canned, sweetened (8 oz.)   104 cal.

Mangoes (1 med.)   48 cal.
Nectarine (1 med.)   38 cal.

ORANGES:

    large   106 cal.
    medium   70 cal.

Papaya, fresh (8 oz.)   71 cal.
Passion fruit (4 oz.)   100 cal.

PEACH (1 med.)   77 cal.

    canned with syrup (8 oz.)   174 cal.

PEARS (1 med.)   95 cal.

    canned, with syrup (2 halves)   90 cal.

Persian melon, (1 med. wedge)   52 cal.
Persimmons (8 oz. med.)   250 cal.

PINEAPPLE, fresh (1 slice med.)   44 cal.

    canned, syrup (1 large slice)   95 cal.
    frozen (4 oz.)   118 cal.

PLUMS, fresh (8 oz.)   94 cal.

    canned (8 oz.)   210 cal.

PRUNES, dried (1 small)   14 cal.

    cooked, no sugar (8 oz.)   200 cal.
    cooked, with sugar (8 oz.)   320 cal.

RAISINS, dried, (1 tbs.)   26 cal.

    cooked, with sugar (8 oz.)   572 cal.

RASPBERRIES, fresh, red (8 oz.)   70 cal.

    frozen, (3 oz.)   126 cal.

Rhubarb (8 oz.)   19 cal.

STRAWBERRIES (8 oz. cup)   54 cal.

    frozen (3 oz.)   90 cal.
    fresh (5 large)   25 cal.

WATERMELON (1/2 slice)   45 cal.

    1 med. wedge   100 cal.
    balls or cubes (1/2 cup)   35 cal.

ICE CREAM

Banana ice cream (1 scoop)   292 cal.
Banana split (regular size)   1,165 cal.
Butter pecan (1 scoop)   297 cal.
Chocolate chip (1 scoop)   298 cal.
Chocolate ice cream (1 scoop)   298 cal.
Chocolate malted milk (regular size)   305 cal.
    with ice cream   600 cal.
Chocolate sundae (regular)   318 cal.
Fudge sundae   330 cal.
Lemon ice   116 cal.
Peach ice cream (1 scoop)   295 cal.
Pineapple ice cream (1 scoop)   250 cal.
Vanilla ice cream (fountain size)   420 cal.

FATS

Bacon fat (1 tbs.)   100 cal.
Beef drippings (1 tbs.)   50 cal.
Butter, salted (1 tbs.)   100 cal.
    sweet (1 tbs.)   100 cal.
Chicken fat (1 tbs.)   150 cal.
Corn oil (1 tbs.)   100 cal.
Cotton seed oil (1 tbs.)   100 cal.
Crisco (1 tbs.)   110 cal.
Cooking fat (1 tbs.)   110 cal.
Lard (8 oz. cup)   1,984 cal.
Margarine (1 tbs.)   100 cal.
Olive oil (1 tbs.)   125 cal.
Peanut butter (1 tbs.)   93 cal.
Peanut oil (1 tbs.)   118 cal.
Salad and cooking oil (1 tbs.)   124 cal.
Vegetable oil (1 tbs.)   110 cal.

FLOURS

Barley (8 oz. cup)   420 cal.
Buckwheat (8 oz. cup)   340 cal.

Cornmeal (8 oz. cup)	120 cal.
Corn soya (8 oz. cup)	125 cal.
Corn starch (1 tbs.)	37 cal.
Soy bean (8 oz. cup)	285 cal.
Whole wheat (8 oz. cup)	401 cal.
Wheat germ (8 oz. cup)	423 cal.

Using this list of foods and their caloric content, you can easily make up your own daily sustaining diets, keeping within the calorie count essential for your age and normal weight. If you binge occasionally and begin to put on those unwanted pounds, go back to your Oriental reducing diet, and then eat the low-calorie foods in this list that will permit you to retain your normal weight and at the same time keep you from being fatigued.